GW00888806

"I SAW THE GRAND CANYON
AS ONE HEARS AN EXQUISITE
POEM, A SOFT STRAIN OF
MUSIC ON VIOLIN, CELLO,
OR OBOE, OR SUNG BY THE
HUMAN VOICE. IT WAS NO
LONGER TERRIFYING AND
AWE-INSPIRING; IT AFFECTED
ONE AS BEAUTIFUL FLOWERS
DO, AS THE BLESSING OF AN
OLD MAN OR WOMAN, AS
THE HALF UNCONSCIOUS
CARESS OF A SLEEPY CHILD
WHOM YOU LOVE. IT WAS
POETRY PERSONIFIED; THE
SPIRIT OF BEAUTY REVEALED;
THE INNER GLORY
OF AN ARTISTIC
MYSTERY UNVEILED."

— GEORGE WHARTON JAMES,
*THE GRAND CANYON OF
ARIZONA*, 1910

# Grand Canyon

## THE VAULT OF HEAVEN

### SUSAN LAMB

✛ ✛ ✛

PHOTOGRAPHY BY

### TOM BEAN · GARY LADD · LARRY LINDAHL

WITH ADDITIONAL PHOTOGRAPHY BY

JAMES TALLON · LIZ HYMANS · GEORGE H. H. HUEY · RICHARD L. DANLEY · DAVID ELMS, JR.

DENNIS HAMM · JACK DYKINGA · CHRISTOPHER EVERETT · JOSEPH HALL

GRAND
CANYON
ASSOCIATION
INSPIRE. EDUCATE. PROTECT.

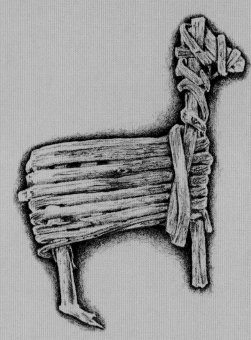

Copyright © 1995, 2007, 2012 Grand Canyon Association. All rights reserved.

Grand Canyon Association, Post Office Box 399, Grand Canyon, Arizona 86023 (928) 638-2481 www.grandcanyon.org
Edited by Pam Frazier
Book Design by Larry Lindahl Design and Rudy Ramos
Production Assistance by Kathleen Bryant
Calligraphy by John Fortune
Illustrations by Roy Andersen: 36; Larry Lindahl: vi, 8, 68; Elizabeth McClelland: 26, 47
Maps and diagrams by Larry Lindahl: 2 (base map courtesy USGS); Deborah Reade: 7, 13, 17, 27

### Photography Credits

Front cover: Tom Bean; i (half title): Jack Dykinga; ii–iii: George H. H. Huey; iv (frontispiece): David Elms, Jr.; vii (contents): Larry Lindahl: viii–1: Gary Ladd; 3: Richard L. Danley; 4–5: Larry Lindahl; 5: Gary Ladd (top); 6: Gary Ladd; 7: Larry Lindahl (left), Gary Ladd (right); 8: Larry Lindahl (top, bottom right), Gary Ladd (bottom left); 9: Tom Bean (top left), Dennis Hamm (top right), Larry Lindahl (bottom); 10–11: Tom Bean; 12: Grand Canyon National Park No. 4907 (left) and No. 17227 (bottom), Tom Bean (right); 13: Larry Lindahl; 14–15: Gary Ladd; 16: Larry Lindahl (top left), Gary Ladd (right, bottom); 17: Larry Lindahl (top), Tom Bean (left); 18–19: Tom Bean; 19: Larry Lindahl (top); 20: Joseph Hall (left), Tom Bean (right, Gary Ladd (bottom); 21: Kevin Barry (left), Larry Lindahl (top right), Dennis Hamm (bottom right);; 22–23: (left to right) Tom Bean, James Tallon, Gary Ladd, Richard L. Danley, Jack Dykinga; 24–25: Liz Hymans; 27: Kevin Barry (left), Larry Lindahl (top right), Dennis Hamm (bottom right); 28: (clockwise from top left) Tom Bean, Larry Lindahl, George H. H. Huey, Larry Lindahl, Dennis Hamm; 29: Larry Lindahl (left), Gary Ladd (top right), George H. H. Huey (bottom right); 30: Dennis Hamm (top), Larry Lindahl (bottom); 31: Tom Bean (top left and right), Gary Ladd (bottom); 32: Gary Ladd (right), James Tallon (top left and bottom); 33: Larry Lindahl (top left and right), James Tallon (bottom); 34–35: Gary Ladd; 35: Tom Bean (top); 36: Tom Bean (top), Gary Ladd (bottom); 37: Larry Lindahl (top), Tom Bean (bottom center), Grand Canyon National Park No. 8801A (bottom left) and No. 8307 (bottom right); 38: Richard L. Danley; 39: Gary Ladd (left), Larry Lindahl (right), George H. H. Huey (bottom center); 40–41: Liz Hymans; 42: Larry Lindahl (left and right), Richard L. Danley (center); 43: Tom Bean (left), James Tallon (top and bottom right); 44: Tom Bean; 45: Gary Ladd (left and bottom right), Larry Lindahl (top right), Grand Canyon National Park No. 4431 (right center); 46: all Tom Bean except top left, courtesy of Grand Canyon National Park; 47: Emery Kolb Collection, Cline Library, Northern Arizona University 568-2324/1911 (left), Gary Ladd (right); 48–49: Gary Ladd; 49: Liz Hymans (top); 50: Grand Canyon National Park No. 4882 (left) and No. 17254 (right, photo by Jack Hillers); 51: Gary Ladd (left), Grand Canyon National Park No. 17229 (right); 52: (clockwise from top) Tom Bean, Liz Hymans, Grand Canyon National Park No. 5117; 53: Gary Ladd; 54–55: (top, left to right) Grand Canyon National Park No. 7060B, No. 5305, No. 825, No. 14711, No. 5578, Kolb Studio photograph/Grand Canyon National Park No. 1462, No 6183D, Kolb Studio photograph/Grand Canyon National Park No. 4744; 54–55: (bottom, left to right) Grand Canyon National Park No. 826 (photo by Henry G. Peabody), No 4886, No. 15609, No. 5972 (photo by Edward W. Murphy), No. 10455 (photo by Nicholas Roosevelt);Emery Kolb Collection, Cline Library, Northern Arizona University 568-3056b (detail); 56: (left, top to bottom) Grand Canyon National park No. 7014, No. 2436A, No. 2435, No. 15523 (photo by Fred Harvey Company), Richard L. Danley (right); 57: (clockwise from top left) Emery Kolb Collection, Cline Library, Northern Arizona University 568-8410/8672; Dennis Hamm; Emery Kolb Collection, Cline Library, Northern Arizona University 568-5787; Christopher Everett; 58–59: Gary Ladd; 59: Emery Kolb Collection, Cline Library, Northern Arizona University 568-7233 (left, detail); Larry Lindahl (right); 60: Larry Lindahl (top center and bottom left), David Elms, Jr. (bottom right and center), Grand Canyon National Park No. 16940 (top right); 61: Tom Bean (left), Grand Canyon National Park No. 12003 (right); 62: Gary Ladd; 63: (clockwise from top) Tom Bean, George H. H. Huey, David Elms, Jr., Larry Lindahl; 64–65: Gary Ladd; 66–67: Tom Bean; back cover: Richard L. Danley.

Special thanks to the Museum Collection staff at Grand Canyon National Park; the Special Collections and Archives staff at Cline Library, Northern Arizona University; L. Greer Price; Ty Lampe; Sandy Cate; and Arizona Game and Fish Department/Wildlife Center.

Manufactured in China

ISBN-13 978-0-938216-53-7 ISBN-10 0-938216-53-8
Library of Congress Catalog Card Number 95-79191

HALF TITLE: TOROWEAP SOARS 2,500 FEET ABOVE THE COLORADO RIVER.

PAGES II & III: SUNSET AT GRANDVIEW POINT

FRONTISPIECE: GNARLED TREE, YAKI POINT

# CONTENTS

"TRANSCENDING THE POWER OF THE INTELLIGENCE TO COMPREHEND IT. . . . THE GRANDEST OF OBJECTS ARE MERGED IN A CONGREGATION OF OTHERS EQUALLY GRAND. HUNDREDS OF THESE MIGHTY STRUCTURES, MILES IN LENGTH, AND THOUSANDS OF FEET IN HEIGHT, REAR THEIR MAJESTIC HEADS OUT OF THE ABYSS."

—CLARENCE DUTTON,
*A TERTIARY HISTORY OF THE GRAND CAÑON DISTRICT,*
1882

EROSION HAS CREATED AN
INFINITE NUMBER OF SHAPES
ON WHICH CHANGING LIGHT
MULTIPLIES THE DRAMA.

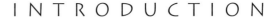

# The Place of Emergence

"WHEREVER WE LOOK THERE IS BUT A WILDERNESS OF ROCKS . . . TOWERS AND
PINNACLES, AND TEN THOUSAND STRANGELY CARVED FORMS IN EVERY DIRECTION,
AND BEYOND THEM MOUNTAINS BLENDING WITH THE CLOUDS."

—JOHN WESLEY POWELL,
THE EXPLORATION OF THE COLORADO RIVER, 1875

GRAND CANYON IS AS FASCINATING TO US AS FIRE. ODD SHAPES AND BRILLIANT COLORS EMERGE AMONG ITS COUNTLESS RAVINES AND PROMONTORIES AS THE DAY FLOODS THEM WITH LIGHT, THEY GLOW, DARKEN, AND DISAPPEAR AS THE SUN PASSES TO THE WEST. DUSTY-SHARP SCENTS, SOUNDS MADE PUNY BY THE CANYON'S VASTNESS, THE ROUGHNESS OF THE ROCKS UNDER OUR FINGERS—ONE SENSATION LEADS TO ANOTHER AND THEN TO ANOTHER, AWAKENING OUR CURIOSITY AND CONJURING OUR DREAMS.

But unlike a fire, the canyon itself doesn't move; it moves us. This is a place where our imaginations are set free and anything seems possible, a setting for adventures of the mind and spirit as well as a test of physical stamina. Approaching Grand Canyon can feel like walking onto an open, silent stage—we know great dramas have unfolded here.

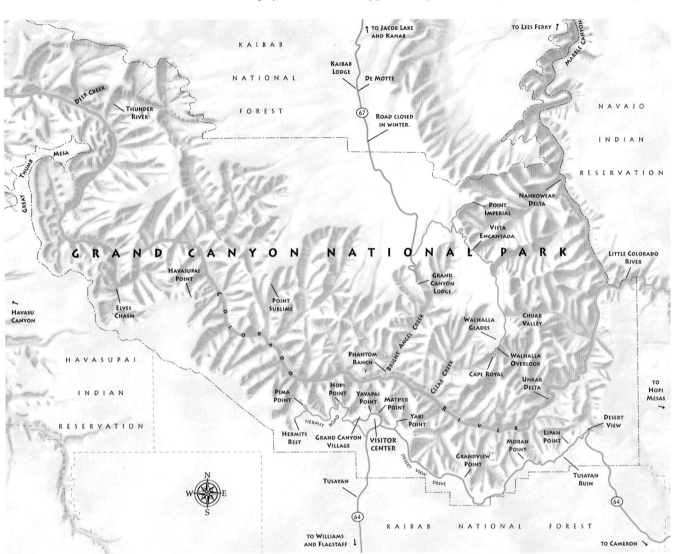

Millions of people visit Grand Canyon every year, yet each has something different in mind. Some seek the story told by its rocks; others are intrigued by the history of the people who have lived here over the millennia. There are visitors for whom Grand Canyon means the wild desert Southwest with its strange plants and animals, and those drawn simply by its beauty. The canyon is vast enough, complex enough, to beckon and reward the seeker in each of us.

Once here, however, we discover that what we came looking for is connected to everything else. One observation leads to another, leaping across boundaries of topic and time. One question leads to another; one subject involves every other subject. And just as the canyon was formed bit by bit, we come to understand it the same way.

I came to the canyon as a naturalist in 1983, to learn and tell the story of the people who lived here centuries ago. Yet in asking "how did they live?" I grew to appreciate more about the plants and animals from the rim to the river, and how the sun, the wind, and the rain determined so much about life here. I learned how the very walls of Grand Canyon are part of the answer, and why people might make their homes in such a demanding place.

Descendants of the Pueblo people who lived here long ago consider Grand Canyon to be where they emerged from a dark and self-centered past into the glorious present. They regard the time they lived here with great reverence. It can be that way for us, too. Grand Canyon can draw us out of ourselves and into an awareness of how remarkable our world truly is. Although it is challenging and can be dangerous, the canyon is inspiring as well. There is something nameless that we all seek, beyond mere survival. The ancestral Pueblo people found it at Grand Canyon long ago, as we can today.

OPPOSITE: A MAGICAL DAY AT THE CANYON, MATHER POINT

# River, Rock and Time

FIRST LIGHT ON UNKAR DELTA
AS SEEN FROM LIPAN POINT

RIGHT: THE RIVER TUMBLES
OVER ITS BED OF BOULDERS.

## CHAPTER ONE

"WE HAVE LEARNED TO OBSERVE CLOSELY THE TEXTURE OF THE ROCK. IN SOFTER STRATA WE HAVE A QUIET RIVER, IN HARDER WE FIND RAPIDS AND FALLS. BELOW US ARE THE LIMESTONES AND HARD SANDSTONES. . . . THIS BODES TOIL AND DANGER."

—JOHN WESLEY POWELL,
*THE EXPLORATION OF THE COLORADO RIVER*, 1875

**O**N A STILL MORNING AT LIPAN POINT, FAINT ROARING CAN BE HEARD FAR BELOW. IT IS THE SOUND OF THE COLORADO RIVER CARVING THE GRAND CANYON. IT IS THE SOUND OF A POWER WHOSE STRENGTH IS ALIEN TO US, BECAUSE ITS PARTNER IS TIME ON A SCALE SO VAST THAT FEW OF US CAN EVEN BEGIN TO IMAGINE IT.

HOWEVER, FROM A GEOLOGIST'S PERSPECTIVE THE COLORADO RIVER IS A RECENT ARRIVAL ON THE SCENE, A FAST WORKER THAT HAS DUG THE CANYON IN LESS THAN FIVE AND A HALF MILLION YEARS.

THE COLORADO RUSHES
OVER LAVA FALLS RAPID.

Because its headwaters in Colorado are almost two miles above sea level, the river picks up tremendous velocity as it plunges toward the Gulf of California. This translates into remarkable carrying power: the Colorado River can transport hundreds of thousands of tons of sand and silt in a single day. And Grand Canyon is just one of a series of canyons the river has carved in its rush to the sea, using muddy sand scooped from its channel and tributaries upstream to grind canyons downstream ever deeper into the earth.

While the river deepens the canyon, other erosional forces widen it. The Latin root of the word *erosion* is the same as that for *rodent;* it means "to gnaw." Erosion nibbles Grand Canyon into towering cliffs alternating with gentle slopes. This cliffs-and-slopes profile is a textbook example of erosion in a relatively dry climate. Frequent, steady rains would shape the landscape more softly and evenly, like dissolving sugar. Instead, fitful forms of erosion gnaw at the canyon here and there, in bits and pieces.

During the long winter, moisture seeps into cracks in the rocks, prying them apart as it freezes overnight. In spring and summer, streams of snowmelt and rain carry loosened gravel and boulders down the canyon's steep walls to the river, gouging out tributary canyons and isolating ridges. The tributary canyons funnel debris into the river in heaps. Turbulent rapids occur where the river hurls its might against these obstacles, creating white, frothing waves that are not only visible, but audible from the rim a mile or more above.

Rain becomes acidic as it combines with carbon dioxide in the atmosphere. It can actually dissolve limestones, including the cement holding grains of sandstone together. As this water percolates through the soil, acids secreted by lichens and plant roots make it even more acidic. Trickling along cracks in the rock, the water hollows out hidden caverns deep within the walls of the canyon.

Gravity plays a part in erosion too, triggering landslides of poorly cemented formations and prompting unsupported rocks to fall spectacularly. As the soft Hermit Shale crumbles into a gentle incline, it undermines the hard, blond Coconino Sandstone. Slabs of unsupported Coconino detach from the canyon walls, forming sheer cliffs. Most of the slabs slide gradually downslope, but some break free to fall with a deafening crash, shattering with the impact of their own weight.

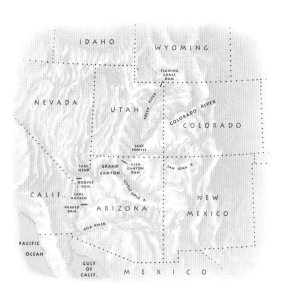

THE COLORADO RIVER IS THE GREATEST AMONG MANY EROSIONAL FORCES SHAPING THE GRAND CANYON.

CLIFF REFLECTION IN THE WATERS OF THE COLORADO, MARBLE CANYON

WATER FREEZES IN CRACKS, PRYING APART ROCK NEAR POWELL POINT.

CLIFFS, LUMINOUS AT TWILIGHT, AS SEEN FROM MATHER POINT

CRINOID FOSSILS FOUND
IN KAIBAB LIMESTONE

The carving of Grand Canyon has laid our planet's history open in cross-section, revealing rocks that tell us of past worlds, of environments utterly unlike the one before us now. In one glance from the rim, we can see the remains of practically any kind of landscape found on Earth today. Some of the layers are rough and sandy, some are fine; some contain the fossils of sea creatures, while others show the imprints of ferns. Grand Canyon gives us a sense of continuity with the landscapes and life forms that have gone before us. Here we are on top, for now.

Erosion and the other geologic processes that created this extraordinary scene are at work everywhere on Earth. Two of the most important other processes are: *Deposition*, when water and wind deposit mud, sand, and dirt; and *Plate Tectonics* (from the Greek *tektonikos*, meaning "building"), in which intense heat within the earth slowly churns its mantle of rock, which then spreads, twists, pushes, and lifts up plate-like sections of the earth's outer crust.

These processes work on the landscape in a continuous cycle: deposition, plate tectonics, erosion; deposition, plate tectonics, erosion. The cycle overlaps itself, too—erosion is wearing down mountains at the same time they are being pushed up, for instance. At Grand Canyon, we can see three distinct turns of this great geological wheel.

The earliest cycle is recorded in the dark, tortured stone of the Inner Gorge. Two billion years ago, these rocks did not exist in their present form, but rather as silty sediments building up on the floor of a lifeless sea. Occasionally mingling with the lavas and debris from volcanic eruptions, the deposition of these sediments continued for three hundred million years. Then shifting sections

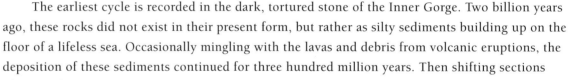

of the earth's crust began to compress the sea floor between its shores. Unimaginable heat and pressure mixed and recrystallized the original sediments into dark masses of rocks called schists. These formed great mountains with roots so deep that they melted and oozed back up through the parent schists, cooling into twisted ribbons of pink-and-white granitic rocks.

FLUTED SCHIST AT RIVER LEVEL

Finally, erosion attacked the mountains for another three hundred million years, eventually wearing them down to a nearly level plain. The cliffs of the Inner Gorge expose the basement rocks of this ancient range.

ROCKS THAT ARE 1.8 BILLION YEARS OLD FORM
THE GRAND CANYON'S "BASEMENT."

# The Sky's Offerings

RAINBOW APPEARS AFTER A RAIN SHOWER, YAKI POINT

SETTING SUN DIFFUSED BY A SUMMER STORM, LIPAN POINT

A T GRAND CANYON, the sky itself is a presence. Here the sunlight is so intense, the air so pungent with pine, sagebrush, and cliffrose, that the atmosphere is almost palpable. Perched high on the rim, with nothing solid overhead and the earth falling away below, we can feel the sky's embrace all around us; we seem to swim in it like fish in the sea.

Although many travelers hope that their visit to Arizona will be blessed with clear skies, it is when clouds appear that our experience of the canyon is most glorious. Against an immense backdrop of cobalt or orange or violet, mist-made characters create a spectacle that our spirits too may join.

Wispy threads of silver called "mares' tails" swirl across the cerulean blue, presaging a change in the weather. Dense lens-shaped, *lenticular* clouds stream by determinedly on high winds. Ferocious brown and lilac thunderheads, sweet buttermilk skies of pebbly little clouds; hail like marbles and snow like feathers; fog like a cloak and rain like a lashing...the sky's offerings are varied and infinite.

We watch as thunderstorms form and move across the land, from their first appearance as faraway specks until the canyon's walls enclose entire storm cells eight miles or more across. Exposed as we are on the rim, lightning is a real and present danger, snapping at trees and tingling the napes of our necks.

Visitors to Grand Canyon expect their days to begin with salmon sunrises and end with flaming sunsets, but a wonderful array of other phenomena await them. On rainy days, water vapor bends sunbeams into multi-hued rainbows. Iridescent ice crystals glimmer on cold, clear afternoons, making halos and sundogs around the sun. The stars are brilliant—their glitter is sharp-edged yet pulsing in the velvet blackness overhead. We can see our very galaxy edgewise in all of its splendor; the Milky Way like a dusting of diamonds across the sky. On rare occasions, even the aurora borealis streaks the night sky with rose and violet.

These things may happen in other skies, but we seldom remember to look up elsewhere. At Grand Canyon, the sky is impossible to ignore. There are many subjects of interest here—the rocks, the river, flowers, and history among them—but it is the skies of Grand Canyon that those who love it can never forget.

CLOUDS LIFTING OVER ZOROASTER TEMPLE AFTER LATE-WINTER STORM

WINTER SUNRISE AT
MARICOPA POINT

# Exploring the Great Unknown

**M**UCH OF THE IMPORTANT and creative scientific work done at Grand Canyon was accomplished while it was still a life-and-death enterprise just to visit the place. In the second half of the nineteenth century, four remarkable naturalists took part in daring expeditions here. They established the foundation on which our current understanding of the region's geology is built.

John Strong Newberry served as naturalist on the Ives Expedition up the Colorado River from Yuma in 1858. He found Grand Canyon to be "the most splendid exposure of stratified rocks in the

IVES EXPEDITION, 1858

world," and drew the first geologic column of them. Many geologists still thought that tiered and fissured landscapes like the Colorado Plateau were the products of lapping ocean waves or major cataclysms, but Newberry understood that the plateau was the work of stream erosion on the uplifted continent, achieved over a vast period. He appreciated the extent of time required by the processes of geology when the average person still believed that the world was only six thousand years old.

Before coming west, Grove Karl Gilbert assisted Newberry for a couple of years at Columbia University. He joined the Wheeler Expedition up the Colorado River to Diamond Creek in 1871. He was of a mechanical bent, and combined physics and engineering with geology to describe the surface features and underlying structures of the plateau. Better than anyone else, Gilbert understood the capacity of rivers to move mud and rock. His work formed a firm basis for that of Major John Wesley Powell, with whom he was to collaborate for the next thirty years.

The story of the American West is rich in sensational characters, but none is more memorable than Major Powell. He had courage, ambition, panache, and a passion for the West, but he was no gunslinger. If a label is needed, John Wesley Powell was a "Renaissance man."

Powell is best remembered as leader of the first and second expeditions down the "Great Unknown"—the Colorado River through Grand Canyon—in 1869 and 1871–2. In writing about these adventures, he wove eloquent descriptions of nature together with scientific observations. He recounted appalling ordeals made all the more melodramatic by the fact that he had lost his right arm at the Battle of Shiloh. "It is not easy to describe the labor of such navigation," he admitted, yet his account is spellbinding.

A self-taught naturalist and professor of geology, Powell served as the second director of the U.S. Geological Survey. He used his considerable talents to further not only science, but social justice. He befriended many Native people of the West and studied their languages and cultures, later founding and serving as the first director of the Bureau of American Ethnology.

Powell's protégé was Clarence Dutton, a fellow veteran of the Civil War. Powell arranged for the Army to send young Dutton, who was still in the service, on the U.S. Geographical and Geological Survey of the Rocky Mountain region (known to history as the Powell Survey) every season for fifteen years.

JOHN WESLEY POWELL, 1869

CLARENCE DUTTON NAMED VISHNU TEMPLE AFTER A HINDU DEITY.

The magnificent wild country of the West profoundly affected Dutton's thoughtful nature. In his imaginative and unusual book, *The Tertiary History of the Grand Cañon District,* Dutton explored both its scientific importance and how it would serve humanity's evolving view of the natural world. "Great innovations," he wrote, "whether in art or literature, in science or in nature, seldom take the world by storm. They must be understood before they can be estimated, and must be cultivated before they can be understood." Dutton began the practice of using names from the great religions and epics of the world for the features of Grand Canyon, endeavoring by use of this "heroic nomenclature" to do justice to the magnificence of this place.

Dutton sought balance and unity. He invented the word "isostasy" to describe the buoyancy of the earth's crust, noting that the crust subsides when weighted down by the accumulation of sediment and rebounds when erosion removes the sediment.

These four men knew one another, and exchanged their ideas freely. Their publications were born of many a shared adventure, many a lively conversation around the campfire. Together they set a precedent for future geological study that was not only a set of concepts, but also an attitude of mutual respect and cooperation.

THREE CYCLES OF DEPOSITION, PLATE TECTONICS, AND EROSION HAVE CREATED THIS UNPARALLELED LANDSCAPE.

Very little evidence is left of the next cycle, which produced the Grand Canyon Supergroup. One scrap of this slightly tilted group of rock layers may be seen from Desert View or Cape Royal; another is visible from viewpoints around Grand Canyon Village. The Supergroup began to accumulate as a sea encroached across the eroded base of the early mountains, depositing gravel and silt. Calcium carbonate then sifted down in a lime ooze, entombing the first signs of life to be fossilized here: filaments of algae from about 1,250 million to 740 million years ago. At times the sea was shallow, exposing beaches, sandbars, and tidal flats of deep-red sediments in which tiny dimples made by pattering raindrops are preserved.

The earth's crust shifted, tipping the layers up a bit. Erosion followed. Then the sea invaded again, depositing coarse materials lapped in from the shoreline and stirred up by waves. Then finer silt built up, and finally a muddy lime, indicating that deeper, quieter waters covered the sea floor. As the sea retreated, this progression reversed itself, leaving limestones, shales, then sandstones.

After almost six hundred million years of deposition, the Supergroup was two miles thick. The crust shifted again, this time stretching and faulting. Another range of mountains was born, but this time the neat layers of sediment remained intact, though tilted at a ten-degree angle.

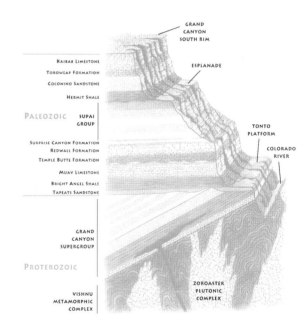

GRAND CANYON GEOLOGIC CROSS SECTION

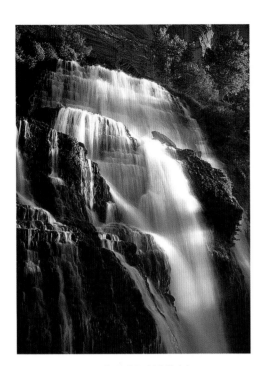

THUNDER SPRING

PLUNGE POOL, OLO CANYON

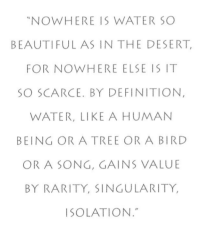

CHEYAVA FALLS

"NOWHERE IS WATER SO
BEAUTIFUL AS IN THE DESERT,
FOR NOWHERE ELSE IS IT
SO SCARCE. BY DEFINITION,
WATER, LIKE A HUMAN
BEING OR A TREE OR A BIRD
OR A SONG, GAINS VALUE
BY RARITY, SINGULARITY,
ISOLATION."

—EDWARD ABBEY,
BEYOND THE WALL, 1984

It was erosion's turn again. All but a few islands of the new mountains were stripped away, leaving another almost flat plain as the foundation for a third geologic cycle. This period of erosion lasted a quarter of a billion years and has the dignified name of the "Great Unconformity," signifying a major gap in the geological record.

The third cycle created the upper, horizontal layers of Grand Canyon, including the rocks we now see exposed on the rim. It began more than five hundred million years ago, as seas advanced, retreated, and advanced again more than a dozen times. Layer after layer of sediments formed on ocean floors, shorelines, and in swamps.

As the environment changed from sea to dry land, the climate also varied. One reason for these climate changes was that the section of the earth's crust on which we stand gazing at the canyon was not always in its present position. The crust is divided into sections that wander—some like to say "waltz"— around the planet, propelled by the slow churning of the mantle on which they float. Two hundred seventy-five million years ago, all of the continents on Earth were converging to form a single continent known to geologists as Pangea. What is now Arizona was closer to the equator at that time. Mucky silts washed down from mountains to the east onto broad river floodplains here. Huge salamanders waddled through swamps lush with ferns and buzzing with enormous dragonflies, simmering in the heat. Depositions in this equatorial climate produced the Supai Group.

Other features on the ancient landscape also influenced the climate. Two hundred seventy-five million years ago, the ancestors of today's Rocky Mountains prevented rain clouds from reaching here. It was so dry that a vast, wind-blown dunefield much like today's Sahara Desert developed, resulting in one of the most beautiful layers in the canyon—the swirling Coconino Sandstone.

Life in the warm, shallow seas that deposited many of the canyon's horizontal layers was abundant compared to life in the near-desert that is Grand Canyon today. Fossils of corals, marine snails, sea fans,

"THERE ARE MANY SPOTS, AND THIS IS ONLY ONE OF THEM, WHERE COMPARISONS SEEM NO LONGER POSSIBLE. EACH IS FAR BEYOND THE POWER OF THE FACULTIES TO COMPREHEND IT, AND NO ONE OF THEM EXCEEDS THE OTHERS. THEY DIFFER AS THE TURNS OF THE KALEIDOSCOPE DIFFER FROM EACH OTHER."

—CLARENCE E. DUTTON,
*A TERTIARY HISTORY
OF THE GRAND CAÑON
DISTRICT, 1882*

ON THE ARID COLORADO PLATEAU, WATER IS A POWERFUL FORCE, ETCHING DETAILS INTO GRAND CANYON.

LEFT: MATKATAMIBA CANYON

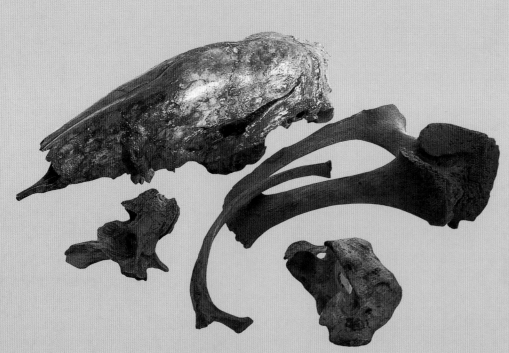

SHASTA GROUND SLOTH BONES FOUND IN GRAND CANYON

VIEW OUT STANTONS CAVE

THE WALLS OF GRAND CANYON are pocked with many caverns, and the dry southwestern climate has made them ideal repositories for evidence of past environments. Well-preserved contents show that these caves have provided shelter to some rather unusual occupants over the millennia.

In 1936, Willis Evans, the foreman of a Civilian Conservation Corps survey team working in the western canyon, discovered a large cave behind a low opening above the river. Clods of dried manure buried the cave's floor. On analysis, these proved to be the droppings of Shasta ground sloths, which are now extinct. Scientists later found sloth bones, hair, and claws as well. The big, bearlike creatures had apparently made the cave their den from forty thousand to about eleven thousand years ago.

At the opposite end of Grand Canyon is Stantons Cave, two large, lofty rooms eroded out of the Redwall Limestone. Early explorers were baffled to find driftwood on its floor, almost one hundred fifty feet above the present level of the river. Evidence downstream around Nankoweap suggests to modern researchers that a landslide there may have dammed the river, creating a lake in Marble Canyon that flooded the cave.

Although Stantons Cave is most famous for the split-twig figurines found there (see page 46), the bones of *Teratornis merriami*, or "monster birds," were found in it also. These birds coasted through the canyon on twelve-foot wingspans around fifteen thousand years ago, swooping down to swallow whole small animals such as rabbits.

Caves in the Redwall Formation also contain the remains of two different species of condors. One species has since become extinct, but California condors have been successfully raised in captivity and released into the wild reaches of Grand Canyon, and, in recent years, have successfully raised young condors in the wild. They can be seen today soaring above their ancestral range.

REDWALL CAVERN ALONG THE COLORADO

THE MIGHTY COLORADO MEANDERS BELOW THE CLIFFS OF COMANCHE POINT.

"PERHAPS IT IS NOT SIZE
NOR THE HUGE WITCHERY
OF CHANGING SHAPES AND
SHADES THAT FILL US WITH
AWE, BUT THE OBSCURE
FEELING THAT HERE WE HAVE
AN INSTANTANEOUS VISION
OF INNUMERABLE EONS."

—J. B. PRIESTLEY,
*MIDNIGHT ON THE DESERT*,
1937

LICHEN-ENCRUSTED FOSSILS
IN KAIBAB FORMATION

sponges, lamp shells, and even armored fish are found in these layers, along with countless examples of what Grand Canyon naturalist Edwin McKee called "the ancient and once world-ruling race of trilobites." Generations of trilobites, thought to be related to horseshoe crabs and scorpions, scuttled in great numbers across sea floors. From the greenish Bright Angel Shale to the gray Kaibab Formation, they endured for more than a quarter of a billion years; humans have existed in their present form for perhaps a hundred thousand years. Around two hundred seventy million years ago, however, the seas all over the earth retreated, devastating marine life. This was the Permian mass extinction, when perhaps ninety percent of marine creatures disappeared forever.

Deposition was not finished here yet, but the layers that were deposited over the Kaibab Limestone that now forms the rim have already eroded away. They were the products of more seas, deserts, and floodplains, and amounted to another mile or more of rock. During their formation, the dinosaurs evolved, flourished, and became extinct.

About sixty-five million years ago, the entire region now called the Colorado Plateau—130,000 square miles of Arizona, New Mexico, Colorado, and Utah—began to rise. Erosion abhors such a bulge, and set about attacking this one right away. We are now partway through this stage of the third cycle. Erosion will continue to alter the scene dramatically, as it has many times before. In the geologic timeframe, Grand Canyon is but a flicker on the ever-changing surface of the earth.

UTAH · COLORADO

**COLORADO**

**PLATEAU**

ARIZONA · NEW MEXICO

# Layers and Layers of Life

NORTH RIM ASPENS GLOW
GOLDEN IN AUTUMN AS
THE DAYS GROW COOLER.

OPPOSITE: DESERT BIGHORN EWES

## CHAPTER TWO

"THE EARTH IS NOT WANTON TO GIVE UP
HER BEST TO EVERY COMER, BUT KEEPS A SWEET,
SEPARATE INTIMACY FOR EACH."

—MARY AUSTIN,
*THE LAND OF LITTLE RAIN*, 1903

**GRAND CANYON'S ROCKS TELL US OF PAST ENVIRONMENTS, OF LOST WORLDS TEEMING WITH FORMS OF LIFE THAT BECAME EXTINCT BEFORE THE DINOSAURS. TODAY WITHIN THE CANYON WE ALSO FIND A MARVELOUS ARRAY OF LIVING FLORA AND FAUNA: VARIOUS PLANTS THAT TWINE, BRISTLE, OR SPRAWL, AS WELL AS PROWLING, FLAPPING, AND SWIMMING ANIMALS. LIFE TAKES SO MANY FORMS HERE! THERE ARE AT LEAST FIFTEEN HUNDRED DIFFERENT SPECIES OF PLANTS—MOSSES, HORSETAILS, AND GRASSES, WILDFLOWERS, CACTI, SHRUBS, AND TREES.**

# Cousins across the Chasm

TWO CLOSELY RELATED and yet different tassel-eared squirrels live on opposite rims of Grand Canyon. Descended from common ancestors, they have evolved distinctive colorings after a long separation from one another by the

**KAIBAB SQUIRREL**

great gorge and the Colorado River. Abert squirrels are rusty-gray squirrels with gray tails, white bellies, and ears that have long tufts of fur on them except in summer. They inhabit ponderosa forests on the South Rim, while their cousins the Kaibab squirrels, which have charcoal bellies and silvery tails, live across the canyon.

Tassel-eared squirrels are one of the few mammals on earth to depend so much on a single source, the ponderosa pine, for their food, shelter, and playground. They are easy to spot as they chase each other madly up and down the massive trees, their long claws scrabbling noisily on the bark and their fluffy tails bobbing wildly behind them.

Throughout the year, tassel-eared squirrels gnaw off ponderosa twigs to

**PONDEROSA PINE, DOUGLAS-FIR, AND QUAKING ASPEN ON THE NORTH RIM**

eat the inner bark, dropping the brushy tips to the ground. We may see little difference between these huge trees, but the squirrels have obvious favorites: the ones with lots of "brushes" scattered around

them. Scientists have learned that the squirrels prefer the pines highest in carbohydrates and salt. The squirrels also know that ponderosa resin can be sweet or bitter, and prefer tasty trees.

In season, tassel-eared squirrels also eat the pines' small pollen-bearing cones, buds, unripe seed cones, and later its seeds. They dig up the fungi that grow on its roots. Occasionally, they eat other plants or even insects, but the ponderosa pine has everything the squirrels really need.

**PONDEROSA PINE CONES AND NEEDLES**

COYOTES ROAM FROM RIM TO RIVER

GOLDEN COLUMBINE

INDIAN PAINTBRUSH

Among them live more than three hundred fifty kinds of birds, about ninety species of mammals, and nearly sixty species of reptiles and amphibians.

Mule deer browse in the soggy green meadows and dense forests of the North Rim, their big ears alert for the tawny, now-rare mountain lions that once kept their numbers in check. Coyotes trot restlessly through the wizened pinyon-juniper forest around Desert View, looking for mice, grasshoppers, or ripe juniper berries to eat. Ringtails—bushy-tailed, bug-eyed, desert "raccoons"—pad about softly in the night, preying on mice foraging in the blackbrush and cactus on the Tonto Platform. Under fragrant creosote bush in the hot western canyon, big chuckwalla lizards munch cactus fruits and bright yellow flowers.

There is yet another, entirely different world along the river at the very bottom of Grand Canyon. Treefrogs call from rocks lining pools hung with maidenhair fern, golden columbine, and scarlet monkeyflower. Violet-green swallows "hawk" insects newly hatched from the water, and in turn are snatched by peregrine falcons. Butterflies flutter along the river corridor on their long migrations, safe from the winds above the rim. Rare razorback suckers feed on the bottom of the turbulent Colorado, now shared with striped bass, catfish, and trout, and with beavers that den in its banks.

Plants and animals that would ordinarily be found scattered all over the American West are close neighbors at Grand Canyon. The canyon is a mile deep, so deep that the rims are often thirty degrees cooler than the inner canyon and may receive twice as much rain and snow. These extreme differences in climate result in several distinct habitats between the rims and the river. A young naturalist named

"IT IS NOT A SENTIMENTAL BUT A GRIMLY LITERAL FACT THAT UNLESS WE SHARE THIS TERRESTRIAL GLOBE WITH CREATURES OTHER THAN OURSELVES, WE SHALL NOT BE ABLE TO LIVE ON IT FOR LONG."

—JOSEPH WOOD KRUTCH, *THE VOICE OF THE DESERT*, 1954

FROM LEFT TO RIGHT:
UTAH JUNIPER, SOUTH RIM

DOUGLAS-FIR, NORTH-FACING
NICHE OF SOUTH RIM

BEAVERTAIL CACTUS,
RIM OF REDWALL FORMATION,
MARBLE CANYON

RIBBON FALLS, INNER CANYON

SAND DUNE, GRANITE RAPID

C. Hart Merriam observed these distinctions here and on a lengthy expedition to the nearby San Francisco Peaks in 1889, and published a description of them in 1890. At about eight thousand feet above sea level on the North Rim, spruce and fir forests of the *Boreal Zone* bristle around moist clearings, while massive ponderosas dominate the *Transition Zone* of the South Rim a thousand feet lower. In the *Upper Sonoran Zone* below that, a dwarf forest of pinyon pines and junipers gradually gives way to gray shrubs and grasses lower down. In the canyon's depths simmers a true desert of cactus and creosote bush: the *Lower Sonoran Zone*.

"Life zones" such as these can be a useful way to look at the natural world in general. However, there are many exceptions to these zones, because elevation is not the only factor to influence what lives where. The degree of exposure to sun, wind, or rain often results in plants and animals living well outside their usual elevational ranges. Grand Canyon's rugged walls, with their promontories, deep ravines, benches, and steep slopes, result in habitats varying from shady seeps in cool side canyons to sun-baked flats. Just below the South Rim, for instance, north-facing amphitheaters harbor shadowy stands of Douglas-fir trees, lively with squawking Steller's jays and chattery red squirrels. Douglas-firs usually grow at a much higher elevation, but the canyon's steep wall provides enough shade to keep the trees cool and moist.

In examining very old packrat nests, scientists have found clues to the various forms of life that have flourished at Grand Canyon over thousands of years. Packrats scavenge a few hundred feet around their dens for plant parts, animal bones, and even lizard scales, discarding them in the "latrines" within their dens and inadvertently preserving bits of local flora and fauna in their concentrated, resinous urine. Researchers inventory and radiocarbon-date these packrat waste heaps, or middens, to learn which plants and animals lived at the canyon and when.

During the last ice age, the Pleistocene, this region was much cooler and wetter than it is now. Packrat middens reveal that a woodland of single-leaf ash and junipers grew along the Colorado River then. Beginning with middens formed about fourteen thousand years ago, it appears that the climate gradually grew warmer and drier. Evidence of the ancient woodland began to dwindle, while more pieces of desert plants appeared in the packrat dens. Today, junipers at Grand Canyon only grow at least 3,200 feet above the middens where they once were plentiful.

The plant communities as they exist today were not simply lower down in the canyon thousands of years ago. The plants and trees of that distant time occurred in different combinations than they do now. Each moment in the canyon's history is unique.

ALTHOUGH IT MAY APPEAR INHOSPITABLE, THE GRAND CANYON SUPPORTS MYRIAD LIFE-FORMS IN A VARIETY OF HABITATS.

MOHAVE POINT PANORAMA

NUTHATCH

MULE DEER

MOUNTAIN CHICKADEE

BOBCAT

STELLER'S JAY

UTAH AGAVE

PINY

PONDEROSA PINE

SCRUB OAK

MORMON TEA

CLIFF CHIPMUNK

TASSEL-EARED SQUIRREL

MONARCH BUTTERFLY

DESERT COTTONTAIL

NORTHERN FLICKER

DESERT BIGHORN          UTAH JUNIPER          DWARF          PINYON JAY
                                               MISTLETOE

ON PINE          WHITE-THROATED          RAVEN                    COYOTE
                     SWIFT

GOPHER SNAKE          SHORT-HORNED LIZARD          BLACK-CHINNED HUMMINGBIRD          NORTHERN PLATEAU LIZARD

BANANA YUCCA                    ROCK SQUIRREL                    HAIRY WOODPECKER          CLARET CUP CACTUS

Grand Canyon is biologically diverse because three North American deserts overlap one another here. The Great Basin Desert to the north is cold, dry, and characterized by sagebrush and saltbush. Creosote bush dominates the warmer Mojave Desert to the west, although Joshua trees and lots of spring flowers grow there as well. The two rainy seasons of the hot Sonoran Desert to the south sustain big cacti and eerie, wand-like ocotillo.

In every case, plants and animals living here must cope without much water and endure extremes of temperature. The canyon's air is so dry that it draws moisture from living tissues. Breathing dehydrates animals just as transpiring dries out plants. There are few pools or springs of water at Grand Canyon, and although rain and snow may bring relief in some years, weeks can go by without a cloud in the sky. Heavy rains usually drum down every afternoon from July through September, but some years they fail to arrive at all.

About a thousand feet below the South Rim on Cedar Ridge, gnarled pinyon pines twist into desiccating winds from the inner canyon, their short, paired needles protected with a waxy coating. Black crusts on the rocks are actually mosses, dormant until the next rain when they will swell and turn green to photosynthesize before they shrivel into dormancy again. Among clumps of dry, fibrous agave and Mormon tea, cliffrose shrubs bloom. To conserve water, cliffroses (as well as mountain mahogany, fernbush, blackbrush, and other local members of the rose family) produce much smaller flowers and foliage than domesticated roses do. After August cloudbursts, the air reeks with the volatile resins oozed by cliffroses to seal in moisture and discourage insects.

MORMON TEA GROWING NEAR HOPI POINT

Desert animals must cope with the dryness, too. Kangaroo rats and woodrats extract practically all of the water they need from their food and retain it by recirculating the moisture in their breath or urine. A few creatures do stay in direct contact with water even here: red-spotted toads absorb moisture from damp rocks near springs directly through the skin of their seat patches.

The sun beats down hard from the cloudless skies over Grand Canyon. Temperatures on the Tonto Platform often exceed one hundred degrees. Many of the adaptations evolved by plants and animals to withstand dryness also help them to survive the heat. Cacti thrive on the Tonto because their once-vulnerable leaves and supple twigs have evolved into a lattice of fleshless spines that protect them from browsers and the sun. They photosynthesize within rounded stems, exposing a minimum of surface area to the hot, dry air, and their gluey sap bonds with water to resist the pull of evaporation. Cactus roots seek moisture far and wide—a prickly pear only five inches high can have roots six feet long.

Lizards and other reptiles are well adapted to extremes of temperature. On cold nights, they lapse into torpors, remaining sluggish until the morning sun warms them enough to seek food.

GREAT BASIN DESERT

MOJAVE DESERT

SONORAN DESERT

CHIHUAHUAN DESERT

"THE TIME HAS LONG SINCE PASSED WHEN A CITIZEN CAN FUNCTION RESPONSIBLY WITHOUT A BROAD UNDERSTANDING OF THE LIVING LANDSCAPE OF WHICH HE IS INSEPARABLY A PART."

—PAUL B. SEARS

CHUCKWALLA BEGINNING TO MOLT

DESERT SPINY LIZARD

PRICKLY PEAR BLOSSOMS

GILA MONSTER

SPECKLED RATTLESNAKE

BEEHIVE CACTUS IN BLOOM

MALE AND FEMALE COLLARED LIZARDS

THE CANYON'S PLANTS AND
ANIMALS ARE WELL ADAPTED
TO HEAT AND DRYNESS.

HORNED LIZARD

BANANA YUCCA FLOWERS

"WHEN YOUR SPIRIT
CRIES FOR PEACE,
COME TO A WORLD
OF CANYONS DEEP IN
AN OLD LAND; FEEL
THE EXULTATION OF
HIGH PLATEAUS,
THE STRENGTH OF
MOVING WATERS,
THE SIMPLICITY OF
SAND AND GRASS,
AND THE SILENCE
OF GROWTH."

—AUGUST FRUGE

A COMMON RAVEN GLIDES OVER THE COLORADO RIVER.

CLIFFROSE

But then their movements generate body heat, which can be a problem as the day grows hotter. Their scales deflect heat, and some climb shrubs to avoid contact with the hot ground or rest in burrows and rock crevices to stay cool.

Three-quarters of desert mammals are *nocturnal,* meaning that they are active at night and rest by day in their burrows where the temperature stays fairly cool and constant around the clock. Deer mice and packrats are very common in Grand Canyon, but are seldom seen aboveground during the day. They come out to forage at night, their bulbous eyes and round ears vigilant for four-footed or flying predators.

On the other hand, temperatures on the canyon's rims often fall below freezing. Little gray-and-cream birds called pygmy nuthatches are so tiny—more than forty of them to a pound—that they cannot endure low temperatures individually for long. They roost together, in hollows inside big ponderosa pine trunks. They usually settle in groups of a dozen or so, but there can be more than one hundred fifty birds in a single tree, arranged in neat rows with their heads all facing the same direction. When they roost together, each little bird can save up to a third of the energy that would be lost roosting by itself.

These are only a handful of the adaptations that living things have developed to cope with conditions like those at Grand Canyon. Each creature, every plant, is a marvel of fitness for what to us can be a daunting environment.

Several animals and plants of Grand Canyon are protected under the Endangered Species Act. Bald eagles and peregrine falcons are doing very well: the hundred pairs of peregrines now in the canyon are the largest breeding population in the lower forty-eight states. California condors are making a comeback, though threats to their long-term survival remain. Rare fish are also in crisis.

# The Arizona Monsoons

MIDSUMMER ON THE Colorado Plateau is a time of anticipation. The heat becomes oppressive. Mornings dawn clear and blue, but by noon white puffs of cloud appear. Within hours, they grow into enormous, purple-gray thunderheads seven miles high. Their flat bottoms reflect orange and green from the land as they boil up menacingly, flashing with lightning, crackling and then booming like kettledrums with thunder. They build higher and higher, until suddenly, fierce downpours burst from them, pelting the parched earth. The monsoons have arrived at last.

"Arizona monsoon" sounds like a contradiction in terms, but it fits the canyon's weather patterns. "Monsoon" comes from *mausim*, the Arabic word for "season." It describes a climate where prevailing winds seasonally reverse directions. At Grand Canyon, winter weather generally blows in from the west, while summer weather comes from the south and southeast.

From about November through March, the canyon lies in the path of winds from the Pacific that bring it gentle rains and snowfall. With spring, these winds arc north, allowing air from Baja California to flow up over northern Arizona. The air grows increasingly arid in summer, rising from the low deserts to sweep over the plateau, drying out the soil and stressing the plants and animals. At last, warm and wet winds push their way into Arizona from the Gulf of Mexico. This moist air brings relief in the form of the drenching monsoons of July, August, and September.

LIGHTNING STRIKES, VIEWED FROM POINT IMPERIAL

STORM VIEWED FROM CEDAR RIDGE

SUMMER STORM DRENCHES KWAGUNT VALLEY, VIEWED FROM WALHALLA PLATEAU, NORTH RIM

THE PEOPLE WHO HAVE LIVED in this region over the centuries think of the restless Colorado River as a living being whose mood changes with the seasons. In the millennia before Glen Canyon Dam was built upstream of Grand Canyon, torrents of cold snowmelt from the high plateau and northern mountains rushed through the canyon in spring, carrying tons of sand and tossing driftwood

**BALD EAGLE**

high up on the rock walls of the gorge. In late summer, surges of warm water, red with grit from the surrounding plateau, gushed into the canyon from the Colorado's many tributaries, boiling over rapids and dumping sand along the riverbanks. In between, the river was a tepid, lazy trickle by comparison. The life sustained by the Colorado River evolved under these varied conditions.

Glen Canyon Dam now controls the flow of the river through Grand Canyon, releasing clear, cold water in an artificial regime based on the use of electricity in western cities. As a result, Grand Canyon beaches and archaeological sites are eroding. Few of the fishes native to the Colorado River in the canyon are expected to survive the radical changes in their watery habitat combined with competition and predation by nonnative fish.

But thickets of willows and nonnative tamarisk now line the riverbanks, lively with reptiles and birds. Marshes are emerging, diversifying the available habitats. Bats, birds, and lizards prey on an increased number of insects, and one of North America's most concentrated populations of peregrine falcons preys in turn on the bats and the birds. Bald eagles that

once migrated high over the canyon now stop to gorge on spawning trout in February and March. These nonnative, cool-water trout thrive in the Colorado River but are threatened by stranding when the water level fluctuates.

Although some of these developments appear encouraging in the short term, such a radical disruption of any natural system can have unforeseeable long-range negative effects. And Glen Canyon Dam remains a center of controversy made all the more passionate because its waters submerged the vast wilderness of Glen Canyon.

Amazingly, some considered damming Grand Canyon itself. One of two dams vigorously promoted in the 1950s and 1960s would have flooded Marble Canyon, of which Powell wrote: "The limestone of this canyon is often polished, and makes a beautiful marble. Sometimes the rocks are of many colors—white, gray, pink, and purple, with saffron tints."

**RAINBOW TROUT CAUGHT NEAR LEES FERRY**

**GLEN CANYON DAM**

The other dam, at Bridge Canyon, would have inundated much of lower Grand Canyon, including miles of Havasu Creek. The protest of private citizens defeated both proposals in the past, and the areas of both dams are now in protected areas within Grand Canyon National Park.

With Glen Canyon Dam in place, the dilemma at hand is how to produce hydroelectric power for the burgeoning cities of the Southwest without further destruction of natural and cultural resources downstream. In 1992, Congress passed the Grand Canyon Protection Act, which mandates that Glen Canyon Dam must be operated in such a way as to minimize any adverse effects on visitor use as well as on the natural and cultural resources of the canyon.

PRECISION FLYING ENABLES THE PEREGRINE FALCON
TO FEED ON SWALLOWS AND SWIFTS.

Razorback suckers and the aptly named humpback chubs (which evolved in the Colorado River between three and five million years ago, making them close to the age of the canyon itself) may not survive the changes in the temperature and turbidity of the Colorado River caused by Glen Canyon Dam combined with the invasion of predatory fish originally introduced downstream in Lake Mead. Fortunately, the Kanab ambersnail—another of Grand Canyon's endangered species—lives above the area affected by the dam. Two Grand Canyon creatures listed as threatened under the act are the flannelmouth sucker (which is adversely affected by the dam), and the southwestern willow flycatcher, whose offspring perish when cowbirds crowd into their nests. Grand Canyon also provides habitat for the spotted owl, the northern goshawk, and the desert tortoise, all of which have been proposed for the endangered list.

Two plants endemic to Grand Canyon are also listed as endangered species: the Brady pincushion cactus and the sentry milkvetch. The greatest threats to these fragile, tiny plants are the boots of oblivious hikers.

People sometimes ask why forms of life that apparently play so small a part in the overall environmental dynamic should be so zealously protected. Scientists offer many practical reasons, among them the point that the influence of an endangered species on the balance of nature is often far greater than we realize. Endangered species are also important as a genetic bank of characteristics that may become useful or necessary in more widely distributed fellow species, and as indicators of the health of the environment that we all share. Nonscientists from many traditions might simply agree with Father Thomas Berry, who wrote: "To wantonly destroy a living species is to silence forever a divine voice."

HUMPBACK CHUB
AND COLORADO SQUAWFISH

THE SLOW-MOVING DESERT TORTOISE
PURSUES A VEGETARIAN DIET.

# Traces of the Ancient Ones

PUEBLOAN RUINS IN CLEAR
CREEK CANYON
ABOVE RIGHT: AN ANCIENT
GALLERY BELOW THE SOUTH RIM

## CHAPTER THREE

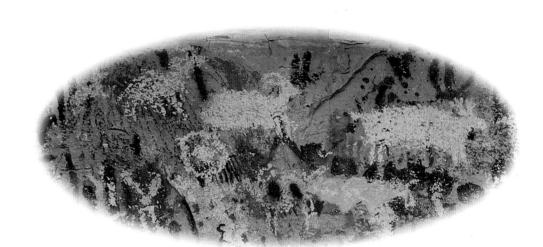

"THE WILDERNESS AND THE IDEA OF
THE WILDERNESS IS ONE OF THE PERMANENT
HOMES OF THE HUMAN SPIRIT."

—JOSEPH WOOD KRUTCH,
*GRAND CANYON: TODAY AND ALL ITS YESTERDAYS, 1957*

THE PEOPLE WHO LIVED AT GRAND CANYON NINE CENTURIES AGO LEFT MANY TRACES HERE. OUTLINES OF THEIR SMALL STONE ROOMS CAN STILL BE SEEN ALONG THE COLORADO RIVER AT UNKAR DELTA AND AT BRIGHT ANGEL NEAR PHANTOM RANCH, ON THE NORTH RIM AT WALHALLA GLADES, AND ON THE SOUTH RIM AT TUSAYAN RUIN. WE CAN MAKE OUT VESTIGES OF THEIR GARDEN TERRACES AND SPOT BROKEN BITS OF THEIR POTTERY SCATTERED ON THE ROCKY GROUND. THESE RUINS AND ARTIFACTS EVOKE THE PAST FOR US. THE HOURS OF RASPING CORN ON GRINDING STONES,

PICTOGRAPHS,
BRIGHT ANGEL TRAIL

ARTIST'S RENDERING OF LIFE AT TUSAYAN PUEBLO IN THE LATE 1100S

WHIPPLE YUCCA ON
THE ESPLANADE

the low murmur of prayers and singing from underground ceremonial kivas. We can imagine hunters calling out greetings as they returned to the village, their children laughing, their dogs barking excitedly.

These people of the past also speak to us through pictographs they painted in rock shelters and petroglyphs they tapped into weathered boulders. These images tell us that they revered this place despite the difficulties of living here. Out of necessity, they were a practical people. Yet they traced fine designs on their pottery and carved delicate lines and circles into little bone awls, revealing that they appreciated beauty, nonetheless.

Descendants of the ancient people inform us that their ancestors also sang, played flutes and drums, and honored their clans. They often slept on their roofs, all of the generations snuggled together in yucca-twine-and-rabbit-fur blankets under the stars. The elders told long stories still recited today in the villages of their descendants. These are so accurate that Hopi and Zuni people making their first trip to the Colorado River recognize places they have never seen before.

Some archaeologists refer to the people who lived long ago at Grand Canyon as the Anasazi, an anglicized word taken from the Navajo language that means "enemy ancestors." The descendants of those ancient people revere their ancestors, however, and many of them consider the term Anasazi to be disrespectful. In these pages, the words Ancestral Pueblo will be used instead. "Ancestral Pueblo" is a good reminder of the link between the past and the present, since archaeologists use the term to describe the culture's early stages and because the Hopi, Zuni, and other descendants of the culture are known collectively today as the Puebloan people.

# The Story of Tiyo

TIYO WAS THE SON of a Hopi priest, who lived at the eastern end of Grand Canyon a thousand years ago. With his father, Tiyo used to collect salt from the canyon as well as brightly colored minerals to grind into paints for ceremonies. He watched the river flowing, and wondered where it might go. After much pleading, Tiyo convinced his father to give him his blessing, then climbed down to the water and floated off in a hollow log to find out where it would take him.

After many adventures, Tiyo met powerful old Spider Woman, who agreed to help him search for the place where the Sun rests in the evening. They continued west with Spider Woman tucked behind Tiyo's ear, murmuring her wisdom to him. At last they encountered a beautiful maiden who led Tiyo to the kiva of her father, the Snake priest. He tested Tiyo's courage and character in many ways, finally surrounding the young man with fearsome snakes. With Spider Woman's help, Tiyo tamed a particularly hideous reptile, which then took on human form to become none other than the Snake priest's lovely daughter!

Tiyo had won the respect of the Snake people. They gave him a sacred bow and taught him their most important ceremony. He married the maiden, and showered with the blessing of rain in the desert, the two of them returned to Tiyo's village to begin life together.

However, their children were born as little snakes who bit the other Hopi children. Tiyo's villagers demanded that the Snake children be returned to their mother's family. The Snake people were of course very offended by this lack of hospitality to their grandchildren and kept the rain from falling on Hopi villages and farms.

Tiyo and his wife left his ancestral village, wandering homeless through the land of drought. When at last the villagers of Walpi welcomed them, Tiyo performed the ceremony taught him by the Snake clan in happier days. Rain poured down, saving the crops and the generous people of the village.

That ceremony has been repeated ever since, to acknowledge the importance of hospitality in the desert, to show respect for the natural world, and in gratitude for the good things that come to us in life. It is also a reminder of Tiyo's great voyage west through Grand Canyon a thousand years ago.

*Hopi artist Fred Kabotie told the Tiyo story to architect Mary Colter to interpret his mural in the Desert View Watchtower.*

MURAL DEPICTING THE TIYO STORY INSIDE DESERT VIEW WATCHTOWER

KABOTIE FINISHING THE MURAL, 1933

DESERT VIEW WATCHTOWER DESIGNED BY ARCHITECT MARY COLTER

HOPI ARTIST FRED KABOTIE

ANCESTRAL PUEBLOAN PEOPLE
ONCE LIVED THROUGHOUT
THE CANYON, FARMING NEAR
VILLAGES, AND HUNTING AND
GATHERING WILD FOODS.

More than a thousand years ago, only a few Ancestral Puebloans were here hunting, gathering wild plants, and farming small plots of soil. When increased rainfall in the eleventh century made it easier to farm the canyon, many more Ancestral Puebloan people arrived about AD 1050, from the area around Kayenta in the northeast. They established hundreds of small settlements, which flourished for about a century until the interlude of generous rainfall ended, and they moved on to join other Ancestral Puebloan villages to the east.

OVERHANG SHELTERS MUD-MORTARED GRANARIES UNDER THE SOUTH RIM

In the eastern half of Grand Canyon, Ancestral Puebloan people farmed both on the canyon's rims and on the river deltas where side canyons spilled soil onto the banks of the Colorado. They had a few gardens near seeps and springs for miles up tributary canyons such as Chuar, Unkar, and Deer. In little plots surrounded by stones to hold in moisture, clumps of corn planted by the handful mingled with beans and with pumpkins that would be cut into strips and dried. Pueblo gardeners welcomed wild plants such as yucca, agave, cactus, and amaranth among their domestic ones. The growing season is long in the depths of the canyon. These little farms probably provided fresh greens in March and blue corn by June, with other crops ripening as late as October.

Probably about ten families lived in the largest river village, which was at Unkar Delta. They knew all about Grand Canyon's diversity of life. Here, plants and animals native to the Sonoran and Mojave deserts merge with those of the Great Basin, making this a rich environment for hunting and gathering wild foods. As the seasons changed, the Ancestral Puebloan people climbed up and down what archaeologists call the "resource ladder"

AN EPHEMERAL POOL

11TH-CENTURY POTTERY FROM THE WALHALLA PLATEAU.

"WE GET OUT OF NATURE
WHAT WE BRING TO HER
MENTALLY AND SPIRITUALLY,
BUT OF NO OTHER PLACE
CAN IT BE TRULY SAID THAT
THE PLAY OF ETERNAL FORCES
HAS SO SURE A CHARM,
SO DIRECT AN INFLUENCE."

—GEORGE WHARTON JAMES,
*THE GRAND CANYON OF
ARIZONA*, 1910

*Traces of the Ancient Ones*  39

VILLAGERS FROM UNKAR
DELTA SUMMERED ON THE
COOL NORTH RIM WHERE
THEY JOINED OTHER
RIVERSIDE PEOPLE TO
FARM AND TRADE. VIEW
OF MOUNT HAYDEN FROM
POINT IMPERIAL

of the canyon's walls. In the inner canyon, they roasted the swollen hearts of agaves harvested on the verge of producing flower stalks in March. They collected tunas—cactus fruits—first at the bottom of the canyon where it was warmer, and later higher up among the cliffs. Yuccas in the Upper Sonoran Zone yielded fruits as well, as did currant and squawbush shrubs in the Transition Zone. The people gathered the pods of mesquite and catclaw trees along the washes, and pinyon nuts fallen from pines on the rim. They shook seeds from ripe grasses for porridge. Fall was the season for hunting, after animals had weaned their young and gained fat, and when the cooling weather was better for curing meat. Men would go off with bows and stone-tipped arrows, returning with deer from the forest, pronghorn from the open uplands, and bighorn sheep from within the canyon.

In summer after most of the snow had melted from Walhalla Glades on the cool North Rim, most of the people living in the delta communities probably moved up there. The North Rim was at best a marginal farming area, but the Ancestral Puebloan people understood agriculture so well that they successfully cultivated it on a seasonal basis for a century or more. They planted on peninsulas of land with south-facing exposures, where the sun was strongest and warm updrafts from the inner canyon lengthened the growing season. Today we know that for every degree that a slope in this region is angled toward the south, it receives as much sun as if it were forty miles nearer the equator. The Ancestral Pueblo understood this too, and planted on slopes inclined about five degrees.

Corn kernels must be moist in order to germinate. Although rain generally does not come to the North Rim until July, melting winter snows saturate the soil there into summer. Ancestral Puebloan people husbanded this

moisture carefully, bordering their gardens with rocks and building check dams in the washes. Ponderosa pines provided shade and mulch, and water collected in natural stone basins could be used to water the plants if the soil became too dry. Because the southwestern climate was as variable then as it is now, Ancestral Puebloan farmers planted almost everything in every place it might possibly thrive, in the hope that plenty would ripen. If a surplus resulted, it could always be stored or traded.

At the east end of Grand Canyon, trails led from many of the deltas by the river up to Walhalla Glades on the North Rim. People from the inner canyon converged at Walhalla to garden, hunt deer, and socialize, and also to trade. Trails from Walhalla connected with Ancestral Puebloan villages on the other side of the Kaibab Plateau to the west as well as north through House Rock Valley to Kayenta, more than a hundred miles to the northeast. They used these trails to exchange such commodities as pottery and pinyon nuts for obsidian, turquoise, cotton, and other goods with Ancestral Puebloan people living from eastern Nevada to New Mexico, and from Utah and Colorado south into Arizona. This extensive trade network even brought seashells from the Pacific Ocean and parrots from Mexico into the region.

At the lower, warmer, western end of Grand Canyon, the rim was more hospitable year-round. Pueblo people lived in C-shaped dwellings of as many as twenty rooms. They farmed nearby, hunted pronghorn, rabbits, and deer, and gathered greens and seeds in the local mix of pinyon-juniper woodland and sagebrush-grassland. On the smooth bench formed by the Esplanade below the rim, they built much smaller shelters and roasted wild foods—especially prickly pear cactus and small animals. They tended gardens in between hunting and gathering in the few spots where seasonal streams—notably Whitmore, Parashant, and Andrus—deposited and then moistened a little soil.

"YET IT WAS NOT THE BEAUTY OF THE PLACE OR THE HOUR, THOUGH THEY WERE BEAUTIFUL, THAT I REMEMBERED BEST, BUT THE PEACE OF MIND, THE PEACE OF HEART, I FELT AS I WALKED THERE. . . . MY MEMORY CLUNG TO IT AS IF EVERY STEP I HAD TAKEN ALONG THAT PATH HAD BEEN SET TO EXQUISITE MUSIC."

—J. B. PRIESTLEY, MIDNIGHT ON THE DESERT, 1937

# Sanctity of Place

**SACRED DATURA**

**HAVASU CANYON**

**SUNRISE, YAVAPAI POINT**

**A**FTER FARMING WAS NO LONGER practical at Grand Canyon, people with a more nomadic, hunter-gatherer way of life filled in where the Ancestral Puebloan people had been. Paiutes—Uto-Aztecan speaking people from the Great Basin—took their place north of the Colorado River. Hualapai and Havasupai—Yuman-speaking people—established themselves south of it, while the Navajo, or Dine, moved into the region east of the canyon. For the Paiute, their lands are the *Puaxant Tuvip,* the holy places where they were created and which they must protect. All of the natural phenomena of the land—the water, minerals, plants, and animals—are numinous: they have a life force within them. Paiute people pay ceremonial visits to the canyon to honor it for providing for them and for sheltering them in historic times as well as in the distant past. They feel that the Colorado River is particularly powerful, generous, and benevolent when talked to and treated with respect.

The Havasupai and Hualapai have lived within and along the western half of the canyon south of the river for centuries, gathering, hunting, and trading with their neighbors long before the first Europeans arrived. The plants and animals of their traditional lands still hold great importance for them, both in a cultural sense as reminders of their self-sufficiency and in a spiritual sense as well. The Colorado River is sacred to them as their spiritual *Ha'yitad,* or "spine."

Like other Native people of the region, the Navajo, or Dine, consider the landscape to be sacred and each of its features to have a significance that cannot be separated from the whole. To them, the Colorado River is a female being that protects their western boundary and the canyon itself is a holy place that has long provided them with salt, game, and plants for food and for ceremonies.

Grand Canyon holds a special place for the Hopi and Zuni people. There are many shrines within the canyon still honored by these descendants of the Ancestral Pueblo, who visit them to collect salt, herbs, minerals, and water from sacred springs. Although most visitors to the canyon are respectful of American Indian cultures, the mere presence of more than five million visitors a year can have a detrimental effect on these pilgrimages and on other traditional practices. As one Hopi put it: "Given the sanctity of the canyon, the Hopis are concerned about the attitudes of people who use the canyon for recreation or scientific research. Using the canyon with a disrespectful attitude can cause serious spiritual problems."

It is clear that the ruins and artifacts within Grand Canyon are not forgotten debris of a vanished people, but rather the familiar heritage of living American Indians who regard them with great reverence. Visitors who leave artifacts in place and ruins undisturbed become, in a way, an important part of this ancient tradition of respect for Grand Canyon and its people.

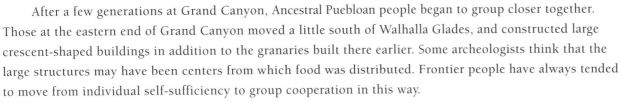

GRANARIES FOR STORING HARVESTS ABOVE NANKOWEAP DELTA

PRONGHORN BUCK

BLACKTAILED JACKRABBIT

After a few generations at Grand Canyon, Ancestral Puebloan people began to group closer together. Those at the eastern end of Grand Canyon moved a little south of Walhalla Glades, and constructed large crescent-shaped buildings in addition to the granaries built there earlier. Some archeologists think that the large structures may have been centers from which food was distributed. Frontier people have always tended to move from individual self-sufficiency to group cooperation in this way.

By about AD 1130, the climate was growing drier again. Pueblo people tried to live and farm in other parts of the canyon, but gradually began their exodus. There was a brief respite fifty years later, when the rains returned and they built large homes, including what is now known as Tusayan Ruin, along the South Rim and in the Coconino Basin just south of it. But by about AD 1250, the people of Grand Canyon had left to join other Ancestral Puebloan villages in the region. Today, Pueblo people explain that this movement was but one step in their quest for the permanent home that prophecies foretold would be found one day.

✛   ✛   ✛

Because Grand Canyon National Park is so enormous and rugged, archaeology here was mostly piecemeal until the past forty or so years. Archaeology at Grand Canyon officially began in 1918, when Neil M. Judd surveyed sites on the North Rim for the Bureau of American Ethnology. In the 1930s, E. T. Hall also did work on the North Rim, and a private group of archaeologists known as Gila Pueblo surveyed part of the South Rim and excavated Tusayan Ruin. A centralized approach to Grand Canyon's prehistory began with the appointment of the first Park Anthropologist in 1974.

"HOW REAL LIFE IN THIS CANYON NOW BEGINS TO BE. IT IS OPENING UP ITS SECRETS TO US AS WE THUS COME INTO IT. WE ARE LEARNING TO LOVE IT, THEREFORE IT SHOWS ITS HEART TO US. IT NO LONGER IS A 'THING' TO BE LOOKED AT; IT IS A REAL SOMETHING, AN INDIVIDUALITY TO LOVE, TO LISTEN TO, TO QUESTION, TO HONOR."

—GEORGE WHARTON JAMES,
THE GRAND CANYON OF
ARIZONA, 1910

ANCESTRAL PUEBLOAN FARMERS PLANTED AND HARVESTED ACCORDING TO CUES FROM THE SUN, MOON, AND STARS.

PRICKLY PEAR FRUIT

GRANARIES, NEAR POINT SUBLIME

PROJECTILE POINT FOUND
IN THE CANYON

MORE THAN HALF OF THE
ANCESTRAL PUEBLOAN DIET
CAME FROM WILD SOURCES.

LEFT: AGAVES,
TONTO PLATFORM

# In Pursuit of Game

I N RECENT YEARS, FIELD researchers have come upon two distinctive bits of chipped stone—both found near a cross-canyon route in eastern Grand Canyon. These glassy pieces of chert were apparently discarded some thousands of years ago by the Paleolithic hunters who produced projectile points for hunting. Although researchers knew that bison and other, now-extinct big game

(L): FOLSOM FRAGMENT CA. 10,000 BPE
(R): CLOVIS FRAGMENT CA. 12,000 BPE

MULE DEER

lived in the Southwest at the time, no proof of hunters from the Clovis and Folsom cultures had ever been found at Grand Canyon before 1993. Suddenly, there emerged a picture of nomads hiking down into grassy side canyons in pursuit of game on which they depended for food, hides, and bone tools.

However, the bison were dwindling even then, as the climate grew warmer and drier and grass became sparse. By eight thousand years ago, a culture referred to as the Archaic hunted deer and sheep in the region. In canyon caves, Archaic people left dozens of little animal effigies, which have been radiocarbon dated to as early as three to four thousand years ago. They made the effigies of willow, cottonwood, or squawbush twigs split and twisted into animal shapes—sometimes pierced with a twig or cactus-spine spear. Then they placed them reverently under elaborate stone cairns, probably to ensure success in hunting. Found in caves of the Great Basin of Nevada through central Arizona to southern Utah, these split-twig figurines reflect a widespread culture with shared concerns and a common way of expressing them.

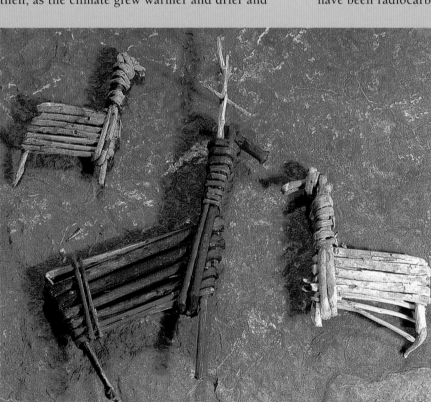

SPLIT-TWIG FIGURINES

BIGHORN SHEEP

PETROGLYPHS NOW SUBMERGED IN LAKE POWELL

One of the most significant projects in canyon archaeology took place during the winter of 1990–91, when the Grand Canyon River Corridor Survey team inventoried archaeological sites along the length of the Colorado River within the park. This survey increased the number of known sites along the river four-fold, to four hundred fifty, and provided a much broader base on which to construct our understanding of canyon prehistory. Most of the sites located are eligible for the National Register of Historic Places, which would afford them legal protection from damage caused by fluctuating flows of water from Glen Canyon Dam.

Observations by many nonarchaeologists have contributed to our understanding of Grand Canyon archaeology ever since John Wesley Powell mentioned a number of Ancestral Puebloan ruins in the journals of his canyon voyages. Engineer Robert Stanton surveyed the canyon for a proposed railroad from Colorado to California in 1889–90, noting a number of prehistoric sites and "creating" several historic ones. Little did he realize that the cave—where his expedition stashed their gear and that now bears his name—contained four-thousand-year-old split-twig figurines. In recent years, mapping of springs and vegetation by hydrologists and biologists has revealed many sites as well. In addition, any proposed development in the park, from employee housing to the realignment of trails, requires a careful archaeological clearance.

Hikers, explorers, and river runners also make important contributions to our understanding of Grand Canyon archaeology. Among these is mathematics professor Harvey Butchart, who hiked the canyon for more than fifty years and helped to identify dozens of prehistoric routes leading from the rims to the river.

Over 5,000 sites have been recorded in the park to date, an average of one site per twenty acres surveyed. The most abundant are sites of the Ancestral Puebloan people, whose occupation of Grand Canyon lasted from about AD 800 to about AD 1200. Most recorded sites are within areas of the park that have been surveyed, which amount to less than ten percent of the park's total area. Statistical projections estimate that there may be sixty thousand sites in the park altogether. Each has priceless fragments of the past that, bit by bit, are leading to our understanding of the many cultures that sheltered within Grand Canyon over the centuries.

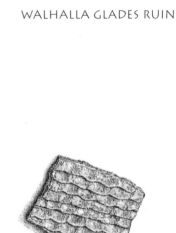

WALHALLA GLADES RUIN

"NIGHT AND DAY THE RIVER FLOWS. IF TIME IS THE MIND OF
SPACE, THE COLORADO IS THE SOUL OF THE DESERT."

—EDWARD ABBEY,
WHITE WATER RAMBLERS, 1977

TUSAYAN BLACK-
ON-WHITE,
AD 1000–1210

CORRUGATED
UTILITY WARE,
AD 1030–1200

DOGOSZHI
BLACK-ON-WHITE,
AD 1070–1150

FLAGSTAFF
BLACK-ON-WHITE,
AD 1250–1300

# On the Edge of Time

THE ESPLANADE NEAR
HAVASU CANYON

ABOVE RIGHT: THE RIVER
TANTALIZED EARLY EXPLORERS OF
THE CANYON'S RIMS.

## CHAPTER FOUR

"THE EXPERIENCED EXPLORER IS SOMETIMES BROUGHT TO A
SUDDEN HALT AND FILLED WITH AMAZEMENT BY THE APPARITION
OF FORMS AS DEFINITE AND ELOQUENT AS THOSE OF ART."

—CLARENCE DUTTON,
A TERTIARY HISTORY OF THE GRAND CAÑON DISTRICT, 1882

WITH THE COMING OF EUROPEANS, THE STORY OF GRAND CANYON BECAME A WRITTEN RATHER THAN A SPOKEN HISTORY. IN 1540, A DOZEN OF CORONADO'S CONQUISTADORS IN SEARCH OF A "GREAT RIVER" DESCRIBED TO THEM BY THE HOPI BECAME THE FIRST EUROPEANS TO SEE GRAND CANYON. THEY WROTE OF IT WITH ASTONISHMENT AND FRUSTRATION: "THE MEN SPENT THREE DAYS LOOKING FOR A WAY DOWN TO THE RIVER . . . WHAT FROM THE TOP SEEMED EASY, WAS NOT SO." AT THE LIMIT OF THEIR ENDURANCE AFTER WEEKS SPENT SEARCHING FOR WATER IN THE DESERT, and discouraged in their interminable quest for gold, these Spanish explorers had little enthusiasm for the splendor before them. They left to rejoin their commander, who was staying with the Hopi to the east. They never returned.

It would be more than two hundred years before other Europeans would see Grand Canyon. In 1775, Franciscan Friar Francisco Tomás Garcés explored up the Colorado River on foot and horseback, along the western rim into Havasu Canyon, and on to the Hopi mesas. Garcés was only the first of many who would wander the region alone or in the sole company of American Indians, enchanted by the land and its people. His accounts mention many hardships, but they are couched in terms of wonder at the richly colored landscape. It is his term *Colorado,* meaning "colored" in Spanish, that we now use for the Colorado River.

Only a few months after Garcés, two other Franciscan friars named Francisco Atanasio Domínguez and Silvestre Vélez de Escalante approached the upper end of Grand Canyon. Originally intending to reach California from Santa Fe via Utah, they had given up and turned south because of harsh winter weather. Low on water and food, they then struggled east across Paiute country north of the canyon, only to be confronted at Lees Ferry by the raging Colorado River. Escalante's journal describes their efforts to cross the river: "Two men who knew how to swim well entered the river naked, carrying their clothing on their heads. It was so deep and wide that the swimmers, in spite of their prowess, were scarcely able to reach the opposite shore, and they lost their clothing in the middle of the river, never seeing it again." The expedition found a break to the north in the cliffs of Glen Canyon and crossed there instead of at Lees Ferry. They pushed home to Santa Fe without a backward glance.

Spanish involvement in the region weakened as events in other parts of its empire diverted Spain's resources. After winning independence from Spain in 1821, Mexico focused on the economic potential of its lands to the north—which included the lands that later became Arizona and Utah—but their trade routes avoided the barrier of Grand Canyon.

By the 1820s, French and Anglo-American beaver trappers were working the rivers of the West. According to James Ohio Pattie's "Personal Narrative," Pattie trapped up the Colorado from southern Arizona in 1826, but had to travel along the rim of Grand Canyon for three hundred exasperating miles, unable to reach the river. Other trappers' descriptions of the canyon's inaccessibility also circulated. Because of such reports, early government surveys avoided Grand Canyon even after Mexico ceded the Southwest to the United States in 1848.

At last, Lieutenant Joseph Christmas Ives led a military expedition up the Colorado River from southern Arizona in 1858, ordered by the War Department to determine whether the river could be used to support military expeditions against the independent government of Utah. After the wreck of their steamboat in Black Canyon defined the upper limit of the Colorado for military uses, Ives and his party turned east up the river to investigate the western end of Grand Canyon. Ives felt that exploring the unmapped canyon was the great adventure of his life. He wrote that it inspired "wondering delight" but was unfortunately "altogether valueless" economically.

After a break in westward exploration due to the Civil War, the intrepid Major John Wesley Powell and his crew of eight plunged down the Colorado for the first time in 1869. In 1871, Powell again explored down the river as far as Kanab Creek, while Lieutenant George M. Wheeler managed to get his expedition's boats as far upstream as Diamond Creek. Major Powell's account of his explorations has never been equaled in the literature about Grand Canyon. His descriptions of the rugged canyon and turbulent river, verdant springs, and the sky overhead leave readers

FRIAR FRANCISCO
TOMÁS GARCÉS

"OURS HAS BEEN THE FIRST, AND DOUBTLESS WILL BE THE LAST PARTY OF WHITES TO VISIT THIS PROFITLESS LOCALITY. IT SEEMS INTENDED BY NATURE THAT THE COLORADO RIVER ALONG THE GREATER PART OF ITS LONELY AND MAJESTIC WAY, SHALL BE FOREVER UNVISITED AND UNDISTURBED."

—LT. JOSEPH CHRISTMAS IVES, *REPORT UPON THE COLORADO RIVER OF THE WEST,* 1861

POWELL'S BOAT WITH MOUNTED CHAIR

"WE HAVE BUT A MONTH'S RATIONS REMAINING. . . . WE HAVE AN UNKNOWN DISTANCE YET TO RUN; AN UNKNOWN RIVER YET TO EXPLORE. WHAT FALLS THERE ARE, WE KNOW NOT; WHAT ROCKS BESET THE CHANNEL, WE KNOW NOT; WHAT WALLS RISE OVER THE RIVER, WE KNOW NOT. AH, WELL! WE MAY CONJECTURE MANY THINGS. . . . WITH SOME EAGERNESS, AND SOME ANXIETY, AND SOME MISGIVING, WE ENTER THE CANYON BELOW."

—JOHN WESLEY POWELL,
*THE EXPLORATION OF THE COLORADO RIVER*, 1875

MAJOR POWELL AND PAIUTE CHIEF TAU-GU, 1873

LEFT: FIVE MILES DOWNRIVER FROM HAVASU CANYON

# People of the Blue-Green Water

**F**OR THE FIRST FEW MILES, the trail into Havasu Canyon is stony and sunblasted. Deeper into the canyon, though, cottonwoods cast their shade and flowers bloom along a cool, sandy stream crossed by rickety footbridges. Hikers soon find themselves in another world within the soaring walls of the canyon, enchanted by birdsong and dappled sunlight.

There are many remarkable things about Havasu, among them the water that flows from springs below the village of Supai to the Colorado River. Milky with dissolved minerals, the water rushes over five travertine-rimmed waterfalls as it descends 1,400 feet in ten miles, through pools of chalky waters tinted robin's egg blue by the reflected sky.

The Havasupai, or "People of the Blue-Green Water," live in the little village of Supai, an eight-mile walk or horse ride from the rim. Entirely self-sufficient until late in the last century, Havasupais tended melons, corn, sunflowers, and peaches in canyon gardens during the summer, and hunted and gathered on the rim the rest of the time.

In 1882, the federal government restricted the Havasupai to a five-hundred-acre reservation within Havasu Canyon. They lost ninety percent of their traditional lands, and three-quarters of their resource base. Although they continued to farm and worked seasonally on local ranches, the Havasupai soon became dependent on work funded by the Bureau of Indian Affairs. In 1939,

DOWNSTREAM FROM SUPAI VILLAGE, HAVASU FALLS CASCADES INTO A DEEP POOL.

the BIA created the Havasupai Tribal Council, which led to disharmony in Havasupai society. As the population grew, tensions also arose over the allocation of limited land. When all of their children were taken from the village to boarding schools far from their extended families and traditions, the future of the tribe looked bleak.

Things began to turn around in the mid-1960s, however. Tourists discovered Havasu Canyon, bringing revenue to enterprises ranging from the tribal hotel to private horse packing. Federal programs provided jobs renewing trails and housing as well as improved education, health, and law enforcement. Reforms in tribal government led to better distribution of funding and projects, and in 1975, appeals for restoration of traditional lands resulted in expansion of the reservation by 185,000 acres.

Many difficulties still face the Havasupai. Sometimes floodwaters roar through the narrow canyon, destroying their homes and gardens. Although tourism brings in money, former croplands are used as pastures for pack horses,

HAVASUPAI WOMAN AND CHILD, LATE 1880S

distancing the people from their ancient cultural traditions. About thirty thousand visitors now visit Havasu Canyon each year, some of them disrespectful of Havasupai property and privacy. A uranium mine near the aquifer for the springs that feed Havasu Creek worries and offends many tribal members.

Still, the people have reclaimed their government and some of their land. Havasupai elders again relate the old stories and traditions to the children, who now attend school in the village of Supai. Many Havasupai who have gone on to higher education and training elsewhere have returned, bringing new skills, energy, and vision to reinvigorate the self-reliant tradition of their people.

CLOSE-UP OF TRAVERTINE LEDGES

awestruck, terrified, exultant, and contemplative in turns. Yet even Powell with all his eloquence still felt unequal to the task of conveying the scope of the canyon: "The Cyclopean forms which result from the sculpture of tempests through ages too long for man to compute, are wrought into endless details, to describe which would be a task equal in magnitude to that of describing the stars of the heavens or the multitudinous beauties of the forest."

Mingled with the imposing names drawn from mythology, legend, and religion given by Powell's protegé Clarence Dutton to the features of Grand Canyon are a number of ordinary names: Hance Rapid, Bass Canyon, and Boucher Creek among others. These names commemorate some of the early pioneers of Grand Canyon. After a prospector accompanying Major Powell's 1871 trip down the Colorado River spotted a little floury gold in Kanab Creek, there was a brief gold rush to the canyon. Although that gold was too fine to be recovered, prospectors continued to probe the canyon's depths for any valuable minerals. Most of these earliest fortune seekers have been forgotten, but a few found a place in history for their peculiarities or their persistence.

Ben Beamer lived for a couple of years in an ancient Pueblo dwelling now called Beamer's Cabin at the confluence of the Little Colorado and Colorado Rivers, where he grew a few vegetables while prospecting nearby. Daniel Mooney fell to his death seeking silver in Havasu Canyon by the waterfall that bears his name today. Seth Tanner set up an ambitious copper-mining district covering a large area to the east and south of the canyon, and improved an old trail we know as the Tanner Trail. This route to one of Tanner's mines by the river became infamous after rustlers used it to sneak stolen horses between Utah and Arizona.

In addition to the prospectors, a few people ran livestock at the canyon in the early days. Cattle grazed meadows on the North Rim as early as 1880, and the Hull brothers began raising sheep in Hull Park south of Grandview Point at about that time as well.

In 1882, the Atlantic and Pacific Railroad completed a line that opened up Grand Canyon to the outside world. The distance from the railway at Peach Springs to Diamond Creek in western Grand Canyon was only about twenty bone-shaking miles by wagon or horseback. Mr. J. H. Farlee built a crude tourist hotel at Diamond Creek in 1884, but the hotel closed after only about five years. By then there were stagecoach routes from other towns along the railroad line to three points on the South Rim in the wider, more spectacular "heart" of Grand Canyon. These routes brought tourists from Flagstaff, Williams, and Ash Fork to Grandview Point, Grand Canyon Village, and Bass Camp.

CONFLUENCE OF THE REDDISH LITTLE COLORADO
AND THE BLUE-GREEN COLORADO RIVERS

"IT IS UNIQUE; IT STANDS ALONE. THOUGH ONLY TWO HUNDRED AND SEVENTEEN MILES LONG, IT EXPRESSES WITHIN THAT DISTANCE MORE THAN ANY ONE HUMAN MIND YET HAS BEEN ABLE TO COMPREHEND OR INTERPRET TO THE WORLD. . . . IT IS ONE OF THE FEW THINGS THAT MAN IS UTTERLY UNABLE TO IMAGINE UNTIL HE COMES IN ACTUAL CONTACT WITH IT."

—GEORGE WHARTON JAMES,
*THE GRAND CANYON OF ARIZONA,*
1910

SETH TANNER

BUFFALO BILL AND PARTY NEAR GRANDVIEW

JOHN HANCE

LEES FERRY

PETE BERRY (FAR RIGHT) AT THE GRANDVIEW HOTEL

FLAGSTAFF TO GRAND CANYON STAGECOACH

W. W. BASS WITH BIG JIM
(YAVÑMI' GSWEDVA)

"I HAVE NEVER WITNESSED
ANYTHING LIKE THIS. IT SCARES
ME TO EVEN TRY TO LOOK
DOWN INTO IT. MY GOD, I AM
AFRAID THE WHOLE COUNTRY
WILL FALL INTO THIS GREAT
HOLE IN THE GROUND."

—MRS. JOHN Z. T. VARME,
TOURIST WRITING IN JOHN HANCE'S
VISITORS' BOOK ON JULY 9, 1892

Probably the most colorful character of that era was John Hance, who homesteaded on the South Rim in the early 1880s and built a trail to an asbestos claim across the river. He worked as a wrangler for the Hull brothers, and when the Hulls received their first tourists, Hance guided them into the canyon. He and William Hull built a log hotel on the rim near Grandview Point and set up stagecoach service from Flagstaff to the hotel around 1886.

Along with hearty meals, Hance served up tall tales spiced with a touch of whimsy. It is said, for instance, that a lady visitor once asked him to help her collect leaves. She gushed: "You know, Captain Hance, a tree is a wonderful organism. It really breathes!" Hance nodded: "I'm pleased to hear you say that, Ma'am. It explains something that has puzzled me for a long time. I used to camp under a big mesquite tree, and night after night it kept me awake with its snoring!"

Pete Berry and the Cameron brothers—Ralph and Niles—lived in Flagstaff in the late 1880s and prospected together at Grand Canyon. They acquired all the mines around Bright Angel Canyon by 1890, and filed numerous other claims in Grand Canyon, including the Last Chance Mine on Horseshoe Mesa below Grandview Point. They improved the old Havasupai trail (now the Bright Angel Trail) to Indian Garden and built the Grandview Trail. Last Chance was one of the few mines at the canyon to make money; a sample of its ore was assayed at 70 percent pure copper, winning a prize at the 1893 World's Columbian Exposition in Chicago.

The partners kept an eye out for any opportunity to make money. Ralph in particular was notorious for staking claims anywhere that might prove valuable later on, filing on a total of thirteen thousand acres— thirty-nine claims in one year alone. The partnership charged tourists a toll to use the Bright Angel Trail

ROBERT BREWSTER STANTON

CABLE CAR TO RUST'S CAMP (PHANTOM RANCH)

RALPH CAMERON

BRIGHT ANGEL TOLL GATE

LOUIS "THE HERMIT" BOUCHER

TEDDY ROOSEVELT, "UNCLE" JIM OWENS (CENTER), AND MOUNTAIN LION HUNTERS

ACCESS TO ORPHAN MINE

and built a small hotel near the head of it. They also built a hotel at Grandview Point in the mid-1890s, which Pete Berry managed until 1908. Tourism was more profitable and less arduous than mining; they sold the Last Chance Mine in 1901.

Three of Grand Canyon's most memorable personalities—William Wallace Bass, Louis Boucher, and Daniel Hogan—first arrived around 1890. W. W. Bass set up a hunting and tourist camp near Havasupai Point, bringing visitors there from Williams and Ash Fork. He built about fifty miles of trail to his copper and asbestos claims in the canyon and raised fruit and vegetables near Shinumo Creek across the river, which he reached both by boat and by means of a metal cage strung across the gorge on a cable. Bass was a thoughtful, intelligent man who sometimes disappeared into the canyon for weeks to explore, take notes and photographs, and prospect for minerals. He befriended the Havasupai and lobbied as far away as Washington for a school and better medical care for them. A poet and violinist, Bass was about forty-five years old in 1894 when he married a music teacher named Ada who had come to the canyon as a tourist. Their four children were the first European-American kids raised at Grand Canyon.

Before Louis Boucher staked his own copper claims, he worked for John Hance as a guide. Although Boucher accommodated tourists in cabins near his copper mine, he was called the "Hermit" because his own home for almost twenty years was in a remote side canyon. A French-Canadian, Boucher prized good food and tended melons and all sorts of vegetables as well as an orchard that included oranges, pomegranates, and figs at his inner canyon camp. He is said to have kept goldfish in the water trough at his main camp at Dripping Springs closer to the rim.

Daniel Hogan filed a claim on a copper deposit below Maricopa Point in 1893, calling it the "Orphan Lode Mining Claim" because he had lost both parents. In 1898, Hogan took a break from mining to join Theodore

"THE DAWN AND THE EVENING TWILIGHT WERE BROODING MYSTERIES OVER THE DUSK OF THE ABYSS; NIGHT SHROUDED ITS IMMENSITY, BUT DID NOT HIDE IT; AND TO NONE OF THE SONS OF MEN IS IT GIVEN TO TELL OF THE WONDER AND SPLENDOR OF SUNRISE AND SUNSET IN THE GRAND CANYON OF THE COLORADO."

—THEODORE ROOSEVELT,
*A BOOK LOVER'S HOLIDAY IN THE OPEN*, 1916

BEFORE THE RAILROAD REACHED THE CANYON, MOST TOURISTS
TOOK IN THE SCENE FROM GRANDVIEW POINT.

EARLY IN THE TWENTIETH
CENTURY, TOURISM BECAME THE
MOST PROFITABLE ENDEAVOR AT
GRAND CANYON.

Roosevelt's Rough Riders in Cuba during the Spanish-American War, then returned to northern Arizona to serve as a deputy sheriff. The Orphan was another of the few profitable mines at Grand Canyon, but copper declined in value, and in 1936, Hogan built a hotel on his claim. (The mine reopened to produce uranium from about 1954 until 1969.)

In 1889, Frank M. Brown and other investors of the Denver, Colorado Canyon and Pacific Railroad Company hired engineer Robert Brewster Stanton to survey the canyon's depths for a railroad to carry coal from Colorado to California. Brown and two others drowned on that harrowing Stanton Expedition, and the railway was never built.

Only a dozen years later in 1901, however, the Santa Fe completed a railroad line on the plateau above from Williams to Grand Canyon Village. Once the journey to the canyon could be accomplished in just a few hours and in relative comfort, the Village area quickly became a popular tourist destination. Together with its subsidiary, the Fred Harvey Company, the Santa Fe bought or constructed several hotels on the rim, built the Hermit Trail, managed tourist camps within the canyon, including Rust's Camp (later Phantom Ranch) on Bright Angel Creek, and pumped or provided most of the water as well as most of the electricity used at Grand Canyon for more than fifty years. In 1906, the Fred

# Kolb Brothers —Photographic Explorers

**B**Y 1902, TWO STRAPPING, adventurous young brothers named Ellsworth and Emery Kolb had arrived at Grand Canyon, looking for work in the lodges and mines. They soon found something better to do: take photographs. Their "bread and butter" was photographing mule riders starting down the Bright Angel Trail. To process these photographs, Emery would dash four miles down to the clear waters of the creek at Indian Garden 3,200 feet below the rim, returning in time to sell the tourists their pictures. Fascinated by the canyon, the brothers explored much of it that no one in recorded history had yet seen. They undertook the hazardous journey down the Colorado River in flat-bottomed wooden boats in 1911, all the while recording their exploits on movie film. In 1904, Emery began construction of the rambling brown frame house perched improbably on the South Rim of Grand Canyon and finished it, or at least stopped work on it, in 1926. Here he showed the movie that he and his brother had made of their adventures to countless Grand Canyon visitors. Ellsworth left but Emery stayed on at Grand Canyon, taking photos of mule parties and narrating their adventure film. Emery continued to explore and photograph the canyon. His last trip down the Colorado was in 1974, when he was ninety-three years old. Emery sold his peculiar dwelling on the rim to the National Park Service in 1963, but continued to live in it until his death in 1976. In 1990, the Grand Canyon Association began restoring Kolb Studio—listed on the National Register of Historic Places since 1974—into a bookshop and exhibit area, ensuring that it will continue to serve many more generations of visitors to Grand Canyon.

ELLSWORTH AND EMERY KOLB, 1908

KOLB STUDIO PERCHED ON THE RIM

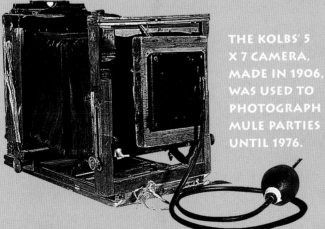

THE KOLBS' 5 X 7 CAMERA, MADE IN 1906, WAS USED TO PHOTOGRAPH MULE PARTIES UNTIL 1976.

THE KOLB BROTHERS DURING THE RIVER TRIP THEY DOCUMENTED IN THEIR FILM, 1911

FOG-FILLED CANYON,
DECEMBER MORNING

Harvey Company began to provide free room and board at the Bright Angel Lodge for John Hance. Dressed in full prospector regalia, the colorful old codger told whoppers to guests of Fred Harvey for another dozen years.

As public awareness of the canyon grew, laws were passed to protect it. Even before tourists had seen it for themselves, the reports of Ives, Powell, and others awakened the public to Grand Canyon's scientific importance while the illustrations in those early reports portrayed its magnificent scenery to city dwellers fascinated by the vanishing American frontier. Senator Benjamin Harrison of Indiana, known as the "marble statue" because of his cold personality, was so moved by pictures of the canyon that he proposed legislation to establish Grand Canyon as a national park in 1882, 1883, and 1886. Mining, stock raising, and tourism interests successfully opposed him until he was elected president and proclaimed Grand Canyon Forest Reserve in 1893.

EL TOVAR SHINING THROUGH THE FOG

JOHN BURROUGHS AND JOHN MUIR AT GRAND CANYON

Popular sentiment grew for increased protection of the canyon. One of its most passionate advocates was John Muir, who fell in love with Grand Canyon when he slept out under the stars there in 1896. John Burroughs, Muir's fellow naturalist, spoke up for Grand Canyon as well. But it was the boisterous President Teddy Roosevelt who could make things happen in those days. First he proclaimed parts of Grand Canyon a game preserve in 1906, then he used the Antiquities Act to declare the canyon a national monument in 1908.

In 1919, President Woodrow Wilson signed legislation that created Grand Canyon National Park. Mining and stock raising would be phased out, and tourist facilities were to be limited so that the beauty and tranquility of Grand Canyon would not be compromised. The Grand Canyon National Park Enlargement Act of 1975 extended protection to the western canyon and the lower Granite Gorge as well as Marble Canyon. With this act, Congress also instructed the National Park Service to study and recommend wilderness areas within the park.

In addition to working for its preservation, people have responded to Grand Canyon in image, word, and music ever since they became aware that it existed. The messages in these creative efforts are many—awe, communion, adventure, sheer survival—but they are all variations on a theme: the human spirit encountering the natural world.

The ancient split-twig figurines and petroglyphs found here speak of an existence in which the starkest realities of the physical world raised human beings into the realm of the mystical. While painting murals in

# Architecture in Harmony

MARY COLTER, 1934

M. E. J. Colter

MARY COLTER'S SIGNATURE FROM
THE PHANTOM RANCH REGISTRY

DESERT VIEW WATCHTOWER

JUST AS THE AMERICAN FRONTIER was disappearing in the late nineteenth century, architects in the Southwest began to recognize the beauty and utility of the building styles being lost. They broke away from the habit of copying European structures to use local materials and themes that were more in harmony with the western landscape and its cultural traditions.

In 1902, the Fred Harvey Company hired a young architect of this school named Mary Colter to arrange the interior of their new "Indian Building" in Albuquerque. Mary Colter's flair for design and her eye for the beauty of American Indian arts made a good impression on the company. Two years later, they commissioned her to design both the exterior and interior of a similar building at Grand Canyon. The result was Hopi House, a unique construction that blends ancient architecture with the requirements of the early 1900s.

Colter chose regional themes for all of her buildings at the canyon. Hermits Rest (1914) is the sort of rustic shelter that a "mountain man" might build for himself. Lookout Studio (1914) resembles a tumbled-down old pueblo. Made of wood and local stone, Phantom Ranch (1922) could be a pioneer homestead. The unusual Watchtower at Desert View (1933) is patterned after the Ancestral Puebloan towers of Mesa Verde National Park and Hovenweep National Monument. Bright Angel Lodge (1935) has the look of a western dude ranch, with a fireplace built of stone from the different layers of the canyon arranged in the proper sequence.

Colter was very particular about the authenticity of these buildings. She employed Hopi and Navajo masons, muralists, and artisans to build and decorate them, and chose the fixtures and furnishings after consulting with American Indian elders and artists. She arranged for the appropriate American Indian ceremonies and blessings to be held at the dedications of her extraordinary buildings.

Mary Colter intended her designs to blend with the landscape visually as well as culturally. In some cases, it is difficult to say where the ground ends and the structures begin. As a result, Colter's remarkable creations at Grand Canyon remain some of the most unusual yet appropriate buildings anywhere in the Southwest.

LOOKOUT STUDIO

HOPI HOUSE

HERMITS REST

COLORADO RIVER IN MARBLE CANYON BELOW NANKOWEAP

the Desert View Watchtower, Hopi artist Fred Kabotie explained to architect Mary Colter that Pueblo people had always sought "to connect the conditions physical and spiritual out of which their art and their religion have grown." He emphasized the Hopi's deep respect for the "unseen forces of nature which constitute life," and how everything from the use of colored corn in ceremonies to recitals of ancient songs and stories expresses that respect.

When the English painter Thomas Moran accompanied John Wesley Powell to the North Rim in 1873, he exaggerated what he saw in order to convey how powerfully Grand Canyon can affect the human soul. Moran spent a great deal of time at Grand Canyon over the next several decades, eventually as one of many artists under the patronage of the Santa Fe Railway in the 1920s and 1930s. The Santa Fe sent thousands of lithographs produced from the work of these artists to people and businesses all over the United States, helping in a substantial way to cultivate an appreciation of western scenery in the average American. Grand Canyon remains an inexhaustible source of inspiration for painters today.

Authors find inspiration here as well. Adventure writers beginning with Theodore Roosevelt and Zane Grey depict the canyon as a noble adversary that tests the mettle of all who encounter it. Nature writers in the tradition of John Muir, Everett Ruess, and Mary Austin emphasize Grand Canyon's power to intensify our feelings for the earth, sky, and all of life.

Grand Canyon is also, as Major Powell wrote, "the land of music . . . a land of song." For centuries if not millennia, music has celebrated its beauty and power. Perhaps the hunters and shamans of Paleolithic and Archaic times sang of this place as the Pueblo people do to this day. Over the past century and a half, Grand Canyon has also been the setting for cowboy songs, humorous ditties, and mournful ballads. Ferde Grofe's symphonic Grand Canyon Suite echoes folk tunes, the wind in the trees, and even the mules. Today, musicians compose while hiking and rafting through the canyon, pausing to play bits of melody on flutes or to record canyon wrens or thunderous rapids to be blended later in a studio or on a computer.

The canyon is overwhelming, and yet people continue to search for ways to connect with it. We feel the fear of our own mortality here, yet are reassured by what we learn here of the continuity of our planet. There are words that resonate in our minds—wilderness, magnificence, solitude—but we are visual creatures, and the sight that says them all is Grand Canyon.

"MOUNTAINS OF MUSIC SWELL IN THE RIVERS, HILLS OF MUSIC BILLOW IN THE CREEKS, AND MEADOWS OF MUSIC MURMUR IN THE RILLS THAT RIPPLE OVER THE ROCKS, WHILE OTHER MELODIES ARE HEARD IN THE GORGES OF THE LATERAL CANYONS. THE GRAND CANYON IS A LAND OF SONG."

—JOHN WESLEY POWELL, THE EXPLORATION OF THE COLORADO RIVER, 1875

THOMAS MORAN

O'NEILL BUTTE GLOWS RED
DURING A SPRINGTIME SUNSET.

"HOW THE STRIKING OF THE
GREAT CLOCK, WHOSE HOURS
ARE MILLIONS OF YEARS,
REVERBERATES OUT OF THE
ABYSS OF THE PAST!"

—JOHN BURROUGHS

PINNACLE BELOW CAPE ROYAL

VIEW FROM MORAN POINT

GRAND CANYON IS A SYMBOL OF THE AMERICAN
WEST, TRULY A LANDSCAPE STILL WILD AT HEART.

OLD AND TWISTED PINYON PINE, NORTH RIM

EARLY MORNING, LOOKING WEST FROM PIMA POINT

AT GRAND CANYON, GREETING
THE DAWN CAN BE AN EXPERIENCE
REMEMBERED FOR A LIFETIME.

# The Vale of Soul-Making

"AS THAT . . . ROCK SUMMIT BRIGHTENED TO GOLD AND THEN SLOWLY FADED TO
BRONZE, WAS STONE AND THEN FIRE AND THEN STONE AGAIN, SOME OLD HUNGER
OF SPIRIT WAS FED AT LAST, AND I WAS REFRESHED AND AT PEACE."

—J. B. PRIESTLEY,
*MIDNIGHT ON THE DESERT, 1937*

**A** FRIEND OF MINE ONCE SAT ON THE CANYON'S RIM IN THE CHILLY DARKNESS, WAITING FOR THE SUN TO RISE. HE'D COME HERE THE PREVIOUS NIGHT DRIVING FRANTICALLY ACROSS A SAGE BRUSH PLATEAU AND UP THROUGH A FOREST OF TALL PINES, ONLY TO ARRIVE AFTER SUNSET WHEN IT WAS TOO DARK TO SEE ANYTHING. OF COURSE, HE HAD SEEN PICTURES OF GRAND CANYON, AND HAD READ A LOT ABOUT IT. BUT HE HAD NOT BEEN ENCOURAGED TO COME HERE. "GET A REAL JOB," EVERYONE BACK HOME HAD SAID. "THINK OF

MATHER POINT,
DAWN UNTIL DUSK,
12TH OF JUNE

5:26 AM

6:41 AM

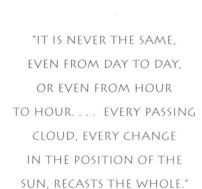

2:00 PM

your future—the odds are tough and your chances to make it will be few." He chafed his cold hands anxiously, hearing again their astonished voices: "You're going to volunteer out there? All summer?"

Well, he would be living on crackers and peanut butter for the next four months, but he was here. He'd pick up litter and repair trails and answer questions; he'd do anything. He was here.

Could it really be getting even colder? And darker? He shifted on the bumpy rock as uncertainty began to creep over him.

Then he heard the feeble cheeping of a bird. Maybe not so feeble—it was coming from very far away. He could see a ruby-colored glow on the eastern horizon, and the sky overhead was turning purple.

Slowly, there it was in the growing light, a sight so extraordinary that at first he could not believe it. A mile-deep cleft in the earth yawned below him and stretched out of sight to his left and right. It was incredible that it could be part of the same, familiar earth he'd known all of his twenty years on it. Yet as the moments passed, Grand Canyon gradually became as real to him as anything he had ever encountered.

This was the canyon's gift to him, as it is to all of us: it teaches us to accept what we think is impossible. It stirs our imaginations, assuring us that the world is full of glorious possibilities. Under its influence we become like children, enchanted by both the tiny and the splendid all around us. Grand Canyon tests the character of all who seek to know it well. With its steep walls, extremes of temperature, and thin, dry air, it challenges us literally body and soul. As we struggle up its rocky trails in the hot sun, gasping for air and water, the canyon's magnificence and utter indifference humble us. It is an archetype of the natural world; in the words of the poet Keats: a "vale of soul-making."

"IT IS NEVER THE SAME,
EVEN FROM DAY TO DAY,
OR EVEN FROM HOUR
TO HOUR. . . . EVERY PASSING
CLOUD, EVERY CHANGE
IN THE POSITION OF THE
SUN, RECASTS THE WHOLE."

—CLARENCE DUTTON,
TERTIARY HISTORY OF THE
GRAND CAÑON DISTRICT, 1882

6:57 AM

8:13 AM

11:08 AM

5:12 PM

6:14 PM

7:25 PM

7:36 PM

7:42 PM

7:52 PM

"THE CANYON IS ITS OWN ANSWER. IT FILLS THE SOUL OF ALL
RESPONSIVE PERSONS WITH AWE. . . . IT ALLURES, ATTRACTS
AND HOLDS THOSE WHO HAVE ONCE GAZED INTO ITS
MYSTERIOUS DEPTHS."

—GEORGE WHARTON JAMES,
*GRAND CANYON OF ARIZONA,* 1910